Tested Public Rela

for Schools

D1168328

Today, when competition for public attention and support has reached an all-time high, the public-school administrator faces an increasingly complex task in his effort to secure for his system the interest and good will of the community. He has the job of reaffirming the unity of spirit and purpose which characterized the school-community relationship of early days. At the same time, he must state progressive ideals and objectives so that they will be understood and accepted by parents and tax-paying citizens.

In order to help him achieve this goal, Stewart Harral has set forth tested methods of organizing and maintaining an effective program of public relations. Since the administrator must keep pace with modern techniques designed to acquire public confidence and support, special attention is given here to case studies of successful projects, ways to gear appeals to specific audiences, characteristics of successful programs, unique ways of making the school community-centered, and methods of competing with other public appeals. Each phase of the overall program is discussed, and methods are outlined for planning, initiating, carrying on, and evaluating each step in a dynamic public relations program.

(continued on back flap)

Tested Public Relations for Schools

STEWART HARRAL

Tested
Public Relations
for Schools

OKLAHOMA COLLEGE
LIBRARY

UNIVERSITY OF OKLAHOMA PRESS
NORMAN

BY STEWART HARRAL

Tested Public Relations for Schools (Norman, 1952)

Patterns of Publicity Copy (Norman, 1950)

Public Relations for Churches (New York & Nashville, 1945)

Public Relations for Higher Education (Norman, 1942)

Successful Letters for Churches (New York & Nashville, 1946)

Publicity Problems (Editor) (Norman, 1940)

COPYRIGHT 1952 BY THE UNIVERSITY OF OKLAHOMA PRESS, PUBLISHING DIVISION
OF THE UNIVERSITY. COMPOSED AND PRINTED AT NORMAN, OKLAHOMA, U.S.A., BY
THE UNIVERSITY OF OKLAHOMA PRESS.
FIRST EDITION.

-B
2846
1293

To Joy Elmer Morgan

95430

Preface

THIS IS NOT a book of one public relations director's opinions. Nor is it a theoretical discussion of untried methods. Rather, it is a collection of techniques and strategies—discovered by many leaders in school public relations, and tested by systems, large and small, over a period of years.

It is the purpose of this book to examine candidly, and in some detail, the whole problem involved in the relations of schools to the public at large. Specifically, it has been my purpose to interpret some of the fundamental philosophies, procedures, and objectives in school programs. In so doing I have tried to confine my discussion to those practices and problems which are a part of the normal life in the majority of schools, in order to provide administrators, teachers, school board members, service employees, and other interested citizens with an organized body of information on public relations needs and methods so that they can strengthen their roles in the over-all program.

This book is not intended to be the final answer—the master plan—to all interpretative activities of school life. Its purpose is rather to discuss and evaluate many of the techniques commonly used in our schools, with the hope that school personnel and laymen—all members of the school "family"—may get a better understanding of the roles they should play in the public relations program.

This volume deals with fundamental principles as well as practical and resultful ideas. It seeks to present the latest methods and techniques covering many phases of educational public relations. Many of the subjects here discussed have never been treated previously in any publication. It is meant as a guide-book for both the experienced worker and the novice. Furthermore, it is a textbook because it presents for the first time in an organized form an overview of the wide scope and tremendous possibilities of this vital subject.

For help in making this handbook, acknowledgment is due to scores of persons. Special thanks for ideas go to the countless students whom I have had the pleasure of knowing in my travels as a lecturer at the Annual Leadership Institutes sponsored by the National Education Association, at meetings of the Alberta Teachers Association, at colleges and universities, and at the many workshops sponsored by state and regional associations. To Irene Elliott, I am indebted for typing assistance.

STEWART HARRAL

Norman, Oklahoma
February 12, 1952

Contents

Tested Public Relations for Schools

1. *Education and Public Relations*

AMERICAN SCHOOLS have extended their mission and services until they touch more lives than ever before. But, paradoxically, many of the "whys" of education have moved further and further away from the public grasp. And as one worried superintendent said, "Schools today face a crisis—one which can be solved only by using effective public relations procedures. Education must justify itself in the minds of those who finance it . . . this is the only way out."

Growth of American schools is one of the world's phenomena. Secondary school enrollments have increased twentyfold in the last fifty years while the population has only doubled. The recent high birth rate means that a million additional children will be ready for school each year during the next seven years. What does this skyrocketing enrollment mean? Just this: It means additional teachers, extra classrooms, and more textbooks and supplies for communities of the nation.

This giant movement started simply enough. Thomas Jefferson cried, "Preach, my dear sir, a crusade against ignorance"; but the crusade was to roll and swell beyond even Jefferson's wildest dreams. Our forefathers passed through the age of the one-room school, the birch rod, the primer, Noah Webster's famous speller, and *McGuffey's* Readers. Ever since the super-charged Horace Mann traveled through Massachusetts preaching the cause of better schools, millions of young Americans have been learning the three "R's" as a part of their birthright.

What is happening today? Many citizens are critical of current educational practices. More than one layman has said, "Officials are continually demanding more funds for schools.

3

Why?" An irate group of Indiana parents organized the "Citizens' Committee for Improving the Schools." Their complaint: Their children just aren't being educated. "Schools are devoting too little time to the things children go to school to learn," stated an official of the Parent-Teacher Association of Denver, Colorado. Many parents have come to suspect that a minor revolution has been put over in the public schools behind their backs—without their consent or knowledge.

These controversies mean but one thing: Administrators and others must strengthen their public relations programs. Education will meet current needs only as the masses of people—the throngs who keep the wheels of society moving—understand the schools and take an active interest in supporting them. Upon the attitudes of the public and its willingness and ability to provide the revenues, the development of education in this country depends. As long as education justifies itself in the minds of those who are instrumental in financing it, the financing will continue. These are bedrock considerations.

Public relations do not, of course, solve all of the problems which arise in education. Nor do they magically insure the superintendent the interest and good will of his many publics. But rightly used and intelligently directed, public relations can aid immeasurably in gaining public acceptance and support—support by which the schools live.

Never before have the schools been under such close scrutiny by parents, patrons, and the public at large. This increased concern for the welfare of schools should be welcomed by educators, because this new interest provides an opportunity for school leaders to interpret their aims, philosophies, needs, and achievements. As public understanding of the schools grows, the citizens become more active in their support and interest.

Most patrons want better schools for their children. They realize the tremendous role of the school in promoting happy, worthwhile, positive experiences for their children. Most Americans want their children to have the best possible education. Furthermore, most citizens are eager to take part in strengthening the school program.

4

The development of a successful public relations program is dependent upon a great many factors. Each community, for instance, has certain unique characteristics and problems. No two leaders use exactly the same types of strategy. So you see that the "how" of producing certain results means that the superintendent must choose from a wide variety of media, techniques, and personalities. Then he must set into operation certain methods which he believes will gain favorable public opinion.

To secure the understanding and support of the people in this competitive age, the schools must have not only a public relations policy but also a definite public relations program. Such a program can be a daily working function of every school, large and small. Even schools without large budgets, full-time workers, and elaborate facilities can enjoy increased public understanding by stressing sound services and procedures.

What the public thinks of your school system is the sum total of what it thinks of the individual parts. That is why better public relations with the public for schools must stem from the work of individual schools and, in the last analysis, from the work of individuals.

What can an administrator do to improve public relations? He must sense trends and anticipate dangers, and he must have an instinctive grasp of the significance of contemporary events. What is more, he must set up a carefully organized public relations program—one which is far-reaching, effective, and attainable. He must make a special effort to reach the opinion-makers: men and women whose ideas and opinions radiate through their groups and friends.

Mere skill is not enough. Back of educational leadership there must be integrity. School personnel must be qualified. They must prove that they are doing an effective job. Actually, the message of the schools must be solid at its core, socially constructive, and durable in value. If it is not, the public will reject it.

Public relations involves more than telling people certain facts about schools. Rightly used, this social science (1) informs administrators and school personnel what the public thinks of education; (2) helps school leaders determine what they must do to gain the support and good will of others; (3) plans ways and means of getting that support; (4) shows the changes in the climate of public opinion; and (5) carries on activities designed to win and hold co-operation and support. In the process of doing these things, it encompasses a great many functions, concepts, and techniques.

Are public relations necessary? No school system has any choice in the matter. The moment you start a school—indeed, before it is opened—you start having public relations. You do have a choice, however, as to whether they will be effective or ineffective.

Public relations cannot be delegated to one person, one school, or one group. To be sure, you must have central authority—some person or group to co-ordinate all phases of the program. That is putting the direction where it belongs. But the performance—the over-all program in its myriad procedures and methods—must be the responsibility of administrators, school board members, teachers, students, non-teaching personnel, and all others who are alert to the potentialities for building favorable public attitudes in all contacts.

Educational public relations cannot live by publicity alone, nor by "parents' night," home visitation, direct mail, local radio broadcasts, exhibits of student work, panel discussions, and the countless other channels and methods. These are vital and necessary, and must be used. But today's trend is toward the community school: one which is planned and directed by school personnel and laymen. Schools and community groups share in a co-operative participation; they work together toward the same goals. Since the public is a partner in educational enterprises, its responsibilities extend beyond mere financial support. Why this rather new philosophy of school-community relations? Because by participating, laymen gain new confidence in their schools. In addition, parents are led to a better understanding of the role of the home, the community, and the school in the whole program of education.

6

This book lists factors which you must consider in building a strong public relations program. But it is up to you to decide your ultimate destination and how you plan to get there. You will find routes which you can choose charted in great detail. May you find the guideposts you need as you lead your colleagues, friends, schools, and community along the bright road to a better tomorrow.

2. *Priorities in Public Relations*

TAKE A LOOK at a successful school system. Pick out the factors—personnel, plant, and activities—which make it tick. Now try to find the intangibles—loyalty, service, enthusiasm, co-operation, and others—which keep the gears of the public relations machinery lubricated. Could you give a one-word summary of your findings? Yes, it is one word, an important word: "organization."

No public relations program can be any stronger than its organization. Without a plan which covers its major points of mass contacts—not just on special occasions, but regularly—a school system is in a constant state of unpreparedness. A well-considered plan gives unity and consistency, direction and movement, to activities that otherwise would be undertaken in a casual or haphazard manner. Every person who has public relations responsibilities must recognize that he is an important member of a team whose welfare—and that of each and every member—depends upon mutual co-operation and endeavor. Furthermore, every person must be alert to every situation whose outcome changes the climate of public opinion.

One of the prime responsibilities placed upon the superintendent is that of encouraging and preserving satisfactory relationships throughout all the various phases of his program. These relationships are necessarily complex, and because they cover such a wide area, they require the collaboration of many groups of people. In the case of a metropolitan system, encompassing a wide scope and diversity of functions, this need for sound relationships assumes greater importance and becomes at the same time more complex.

These are momentous days in school public relations programs. Parents and other interested persons are showing a renewed desire to participate. They want to have a part in discussing, suggesting, changing, and approving policies that are to be used in their schools. They know that lay interest must accompany every step in the progress of education. On every hand they are saying, "Let us help." With the schools facing a new crisis, perhaps the most vital one in history, more and more superintendents are asking, "How can we step up the effectiveness of our public relations without increasing expenses? How can we make the most of our staff and facilities?"

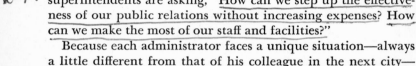

Because each administrator faces a unique situation—always a little different from that of his colleague in the next city—there cannot be stock answers to problems of organization. Merely copying another's program is no solution, for what is sure-fire in one situation may be disastrous in another. Each superintendent must develop his own setup, tailor-made to fit the needs of his particular operation.

Too many school heads have avoided any strict organizational plan because they have believed that it would require a large staff and a huge budget. Obviously, this is a misconception, one which is fading as more school leaders realize that they can make the most of what they have, both in staff and in financial support. Actually, there are many types of organizations which range from a staff of full-time workers to the simple yet effective system in which many people—staff, parents, teachers, and students—are utilized on a voluntary basis.

Typical setups follow: (1) the superintendent may carry most of the load; (2) a full-time or part-time person may direct the program; (3) most of the authority may be delegated to the principals; (4) a central committee of eight or ten members may be named, composed of teachers and principals; or (5) a city-wide committee may be named, composed of both school personnel and laymen, which acts as an advisory council to the

8

superintendent. The local situation will always determine to a marked degree what plan is followed.

Whatever type of organization is used, authority must be delegated to some person who is skilled in guiding human relations. By virtue of his position, the superintendent is the executive head of the program. To the public at large, he is the symbol of all the schools, of their problems, philosophies, activities, and achievements. As a leader, the superintendent shows the way and makes suggestions while he himself often remains in the background, "building up" as many staff members as possible. As one said, "I try to keep in the background much of the time and run the school system in a co-operative manner. It's the old idea of teamwork. Each person must be made to feel that he is a member of a team—a team that wants to win."

The superintendent needs the support of many people and many publics. Together with the principals, he can enlist not only the aid of students and teachers, but also parent-teacher groups, mothers' clubs, civic groups, and many others. Nothing is more effective in building better public relations than programs planned jointly by the school and the community.

How effective is the part-time public relations worker? His effectiveness is dependent upon a number of factors. Generally speaking, he cannot function too successfully because so many emergencies occur in public contacts. He may be teaching or doing other work when something vital happens in public relations. If possible, he should have an assistant who has the authority to make decisions. Whatever the size of the system, the part-time worker should not be overloaded. His duties and responsibilities should be made known to all. When this is done, he isn't so likely to become an "errand-boy" for many persons and groups.

Whether full- or part-time, the person chosen for the assignment must work side by side with the superintendent in determining the policy of the system. The superintendent must have a sympathetic ear for public relations problems and must set aside time to consider them. Above all, he must have confidence and faith in those delegated to carry out specific func-

9

tions. It is essential that public relations workers, whether they are full-time, part-time, or volunteers, be allowed reasonable latitude—always within the limits of school policy, of course.

When a public relations committee is chosen, the superintendent should exercise great care in the selection of members. If possible, he should choose members on the basis of their interests and special abilities. If a speakers' bureau is one phase of the program, then a teacher whose interest lies in this area should be named. If an all-school exhibit is planned, talent for this type of work should be sought. The wise superintendent thinks in terms of his over-all program and selects committee members who will be representative of many interests. The size of the group will be determined by the nature of the proposed program, its immediate importance, the size of the system, and other factors. In any event, the committee should be organized so that no individual will have too much of a load.

No matter what organizational structure is used, all persons associated with the schools—administrators, principals, teachers, students, and parents—must be active agents in building good will and co-operation. Naming a full-time or part-time director or setting up a committee places the direction where it belongs. But results will come only when all persons and groups perform their duties so that public acceptance increases.

ELEMENTS OF A SCHOOL PUBLIC RELATIONS PROGRAM[1]

Preliminary requirements:

1. There must be an earnest and sincere desire on the part of the administration and staff to improve public relations. Public relations begin at home.

2. Past policies and procedures must be examined in the light of their contribution toward increased good will, understanding, and support.

3. Causes of ill will and misunderstanding between the school system and its supporting publics must be removed.

[1] Adapted from *Public Relations for Higher Education,* by Stewart Harral (Norman, University of Oklahoma Press, 1942), 266–67.

4. Dissension and friction within the system must be cleared up.

5. Every staff member must be educated both to his responsibilities and to his limitations in the public relations program.

Leadership—Organization:

1. Leadership must be delegated to an able person (or committee) who has knowledge of the most effective procedures and who is skilled in guiding human relations.

2. The organization must be set up so that its functions and activities are clearly defined and so that the authority and responsibility are known to all.

3. The director of public relations should have the complete confidence of the administration, the staff, and the public, and should know fully the background of the system.

Policies—Procedures:

1. A basic yet flexible program of policies must be defined and set in operation.

2. Every policy, no matter what phase of the program it is to govern, must be formulated and carried out in relation to its effect on all institutional publics—administrators, teachers, employees, graduates, the board of education, and the public at large.

3. The superintendent must constantly strengthen those institutional influences which increase the efficiency and loyalty of the personnel.

4. As far as possible, all procedures should be carried out in such a way that they will win public approval.

5. All methods and procedures should be so designed that they will strictly conform to the public relations policies. Consistency in following policies will remove any doubt or question of sincerity.

6. The director of public relations or the superintendent must analyze each problem in its relationship to the basic motivations of those groups upon whose good will the institution is dependent.

7. Every procedure should be designed in the public interest, because ideas that are not generally accepted by the public be-

come so only after it is shown that they are of value and interest to the public.

8. Two-way communication—both sending and receiving—must be maintained at all times between the administrator and personnel and between all institutional agencies and their publics.

9. Frequent studies should be made to reveal any fundamental changes that are taking place in public opinion, so that the institution may get a better perspective of its activities and services.

10. By continuous use of all channels and media, every segment of the public should be given a full, frank, authoritative account of institutional policies, activities, objectives, and needs.

1. All ideas and objectives must be translated into the language and interests of those to be reached, so that a favorable reception results.

12. Recognition must be made of the fact that public relations activities are not to be reserved for special occasions, but must function in normal day-to-day relationships.

13. As much as possible, an attempt must be made to acquaint all publics thoroughly with the system and thus make its interests of deep concern to them.

3. *Guides to Opinion Polls*

PUBLIC RELATIONS are based on facts. School leaders should make a choice of devices and procedures only after the facts are known. "It never pays to gamble in a long-range campaign," one superintendent said, "because the schools' investments and future are at stake. Time or money spent in research —fact finding, opinion polls—are good insurance."

Every public relations situation begins with a careful study of all the underlying facts. The superintendent does not rely merely on the beliefs of an individual or group, but gets his information from every available source. The more information he has, the more he can reduce the element of chance in his planning and strategies.

Fact-finding demands checking and double checking. The superintendent searches for omissions and errors; he analyzes every element that applies to the particular situation. In this way he may run across some factor which the opposition may wish to have and use with profit against him. This is important, because as Karl E. Ettinger, public relations and research counselor, reminds us, "Solving a public relations problem depends on seeing one's weaknesses before opposing forces become aware of them."

Armed with facts, a superintendent is protected against surprise. Like the lawyer, he must be prepared not merely to speak in defense of an individual or institution, but to promote it. The more the superintendent knows about public attitudes the more he can adjust policies and actions so that they will convey the desired impression to the public mind. Let's remember that public relations objectives start with the public and not with the schools. Many persons and institutions have learned the value of knowing "what's on the public's mind" and then of using that information in a practical way.

The school system is the largest undertaking in the community. It is owned by the people. Their knowledge of the aims and problems of the school system is a vital factor in their support or lack of support. That is why scientific polling can be of immense value to the administrator when he wishes to know how citizens feel toward the community educational program.

The poll can become a fundamental tool of school administration because:

1. it reveals areas of ignorance and misinformation, as well as the success of the public relations program in enlightening such areas;

2. it informs and instructs the community on educational issues;

3. it supplies the superintendent with essential information

about the prevailing opinions and attitudes on educational matters, both favorable and unfavorable;

4. it allows the administrator to see the extent of the lag between the program he is proposing and the one the citizens support;

5. it gives the community a sense of sharing in problems, philosophies, and plans of the school system;

6. it often reveals clearly-defined obstacles which the administrator must overcome before the people are sold on certain ideas and proposals;

7. it can find out quickly and accurately the view of any group in a community.

Whatever type of poll is used, be sure that careful plans are made concerning questions to be asked, people to be surveyed, timing, and analysis.
Typical questions might be:

1. Are you, in general, satisfied with the way our schools are run?

2. Do you think that all school children should receive complete physical examinations by doctors every two or three years?

3. What do you think the school system should reasonably do for its students which it is not now doing?

4. Do you think that high school teachers should discuss all forms of national government in their classes?

5. What feature do you like best about our schools?
Follow fact-finding with analysis:

1. Report results of the survey to the board of education.

2. Clear up or reduce the unfavorable aspects of the program.

3. Use the findings to modify your program and policies.

4. Capitalize on the strengths of the program.

Mail surveys are used in many school systems. They are inexpensive and do not require the large staff which is necessary in field work. Furthermore, some people will respond to mail questionnaires more willingly than they will answer questions of interviewers. If respondents are anonymous, they are more likely to give a frank statement of opinions. Of course, sampling opinion by mail has its hazards. Some to whom forms have been sent may not be interested enough to return them, and real danger lies in interpreting facts from the few questionnaires which were returned. What were the attitudes of those who did not respond?

Often a school system in a metropolitan city contracts with an independent research organization to make its survey. This was done, for example, in Denver, Colorado, and the booklet, *Denver Looks at Its Schools,* presented the findings of the inquiry.

This project, which was conducted by Research Services, Inc., of Denver, in consultation with the National Opinion Research Center of the University of Illinois, was made because "it is essential to know the opinions of large numbers of citizens if we are to develop properly a vital public education program." Personal interviews were held with 1,011 adults selected at random, and 250 Denver public school teachers, similarly chosen, were mailed questionnaires to which they replied anonymously. Two subjects were paramount in the survey: the attitude toward the current progress of the Denver public schools, and public needs and expectations with regard to the curriculum.

In announcing the survey, officials of the board of education stated, "It has always been our philosophy that a school draws its strengths or weaknesses in a large part from the community which it serves and that the concept in the minds of our citizens of what a good school looks like plays a vital part in determining the power of the educational program in Denver. In building our courses of study, we have always taken into account the thinking of the people of this city; and the decision to conduct this scientific survey of public opinion is evidence of our genuine interest in what the people think about their schools."

Even though scientific polling is still in its formative stages, it has proceeded far enough that we can measure public attitudes with a high degree of accuracy. No school, regardless of its size, can afford not to study public attitudes and use opinion surveys as the basis of sound planning in public relations. Moreover, school executives must not rely on occasional surveys.

Rather, they should pattern themselves after industrial leaders and others who follow trends in public opinion in a wide variety of continuing studies.

4. *Winning Community Confidence*

EVERY SUPERINTENDENT is inclined at times to be infatuated with the sound of his own facts, figures, and achievements. He may be so close to his situation that he has no idea how his work is regarded by the general public. He may be taking favorable public opinion for granted. The most accurately compiled figures from the local school survey cannot tell the whole story of what is on the public mind. And, too, they have a way of cooling off and losing some of their meaning before they are analyzed and published. They are important; but often the intangibles—why and how strongly people feel as they do toward the school system—are most important.

The question is asked frequently, "What is the first step in public relations?" First of all, the public relations worker must determine what people think about the schools today—not last year nor the first day of school last September, but *today*.

The wise superintendent will welcome any device or method that will enable him to appraise attitudes of the public (teachers, students, parents, community leaders, and so on) toward the system. Reliable opinion data must be compiled at regular intervals if the schools are to be judged accurately. Get all the facts and opinions which are available. Then analyze the findings and put them to use. By this process the school head may discover mistakes that have been made and the reasons for them. He can detect common misconceptions which may exist regarding the schools, and he can determine where progress has been made.

Now, of course, he will get many opinions which must be taken with a grain of salt. He must remember, however, that untrue as they may be, they do exist. When all of the evidence is in, the superintendent will at least know the "what" and the "how much" of certain attitudes. Being aware of these opinions, he can proceed more intelligently and effectively than the old method of "shooting in the dark" permitted.

More and more school systems are making greater use of their personnel as reporting agents on matters of public opinion. It may be a bitter dose to some superintendents, but the plan of asking associates who are close to the public mind to record all the criticisms they have heard will bring in pertinent comments. This type of sampling cannot be labeled as either scientific or complete, but it is practical as far as it goes.

After an analysis of the problem, objectives must be decided upon. Suppose a survey shows that 60 per cent of the parents polled believe that less than half the subjects their children are studying in high school will be valuable in real life. This result would certainly give the staff a target in public relations.

Once the objectives are planned, careful thought must be given to ways of changing the opinion or counteracting it. Suppose, for example, that a significant number of parents think that home-school relations might be improved. To remedy this situation, the superintendent might launch a new visitation program, invite more parents to school affairs, project certain ideas through P.T.A. leaders, do a series of letters to parents, and start other worthwhile activities.

Knowing at what level to focus a public relations procedure is at once a tremendously important and knotty problem. It is quite as easy to underestimate the intelligence of a group as it is to overestimate it. In dealing with mass opinions, we must not forget that over the last few decades the American public has become one of the best informed in the world. Even in making a trial approach, the superintendent should guard against aiming his efforts at too low a mental level.

Every school representative—teacher, secretary, principal, nurse, custodian, and student—must be educated both to his responsibilities and to his limitations in the public relations program. Each worker should know the nature of his task and how it fits into the plan as a whole. It does not cost the administrator much in time or effort to adopt a friendly attitude toward all essential helpers. By doing so, he gives social recognition to the persons and their work. They will generally respond better to the job and find helpful things to do. No one can overestimate the importance of having intelligently informed personnel, friendly to the school's manifold public, acting as contact agents. To be successful, the public relations program must be valued by all persons who work for its realization.

As the plan of action gets under way, it is well to remember that the principal characteristics of a public relations program are that it should be:

1. Attainable—there's no use shooting for the moon.
2. Continuous—repetition is reputation.
3. Ethical—tell the whole truth and nothing but the truth.
4. Interesting—plan a program that will catch attention.
5. Progressive—stay out of the rut if you're going any place.
6. Dynamic—workers and volunteers must be enthusiastic and optimistic.
7. Comprehensive—use all available channels to reach the public concerned.
8. Two-way—administrators must get across certain ideas and yet must be sensitive to what the public is thinking.
9. Balanced—all phases must be given proper time and emphasis.
10. Administrative—public relations functions must be at the policy-making level.
11. Planned—every step must be charted.
12. Guided—leadership is fundamental in effective public relations.
13. Timely—the program must be geared to current situations.
14. Inclusive—a carefully planned program reaches all segments of the public upon whose support the schools depend.
15. Flexible—procedure should be planned so that a variety of approaches may be used.

In a public relations campaign the main problem may arise

after the work is under way and the first difficulties appear on the horizon. A plan which seemed perfect at a meeting of the all-school public relations committee may fall with a crash when it meets reality. Some setbacks may be avoided if the superintendent can anticipate (1) adverse reactions to his program, (2) the intensity of the criticism, (3) the nature of the criticism (whether it is recurrent or is coming to light for the first time), and (4) causes of the negative reaction. By foreseeing certain objections, the superintendent can have his answers ready. If these are acceptable to the public, then the institutional policies can be brought into closer harmony with public opinion.

Any policy, no matter to what area or subject it will apply, should be formed and carried out in relation to its effect on all elements of your public—staff, parents, civic groups, students, and others.

Generally, there are two types of policies. One is made for a long-term program and varies little through the weeks or years. For instance, you have discovered that an orientation course is a valuable public relations practice for new secretaries and other office workers. You believe the idea worth while because it has shown results in every system you have served. Then there is the short-term policy which is made to help in an emergency. For example, you appoint a committee to plan a dinner honoring present and former members of the school board. With its responsibilities ended, the group disbands following the event.

As far as possible, all procedures should be carried out in such a way as to win public approval. Just as we can "rub a person the wrong way," so we can do things which offend the public. Under ordinary conditions, it is wise for the school head to advance his ideas in a manner that invites agreement, not with the cocksure approach that provokes argument and opposition.

In every instance, the superintendent or persons directly responsible must analyze each problem in its relationship to the basic motivations of those groups upon whose good will the schools are dependent. The newest trend in public relations is to get schools and community groups working together toward the same goals. When there is a common concern for community well-being, schools will be adequately supported. No two communities are exactly alike. One may differ from another in physical attributes—in size, location, and number of inhabitants. And yet, each seeks to be the kind of place in which children may live richly and grow to the full stature of free men and women. As the superintendent analyzes his local situation, he must understand its uniqueness, its people, its needs, and then carefully plan a program of community-school co-operation. By all means, these programs should be continuous and should avoid the appearance of drives or high-pressure campaigns.

Two-way communication should be maintained at all times between the school head and his personnel, and between all school agencies and their publics. Often a superintendent says, "I've lost touch with my people." Close planning and co-operation are necessary at all stages between the school and public. It isn't enough that public relations merely interpret. Nor can they emphasize and do nothing else. Public confidence will come when teachers and laymen are made active partners in improving educational policy.

5. *Tuning Ideas to the Proper Key*

BEFORE your public relations program can win friends, it must be tuned to the right key. That is why it is important to know at what level to direct your messages, to know how your ideas can be geared to those of the supporting public —in other words, to know how to synchronize your efforts with the public mind.

Like the expert salesman, the public relations practitioner not only must know his idea or proposal well, but must know his prospects better. If he has more than one audience, he can plan a special approach for each. Many a public relations program misses the mark because some person has fired before anyone saw the target.

Unless you know your public, your efforts will be aimless and ineffective. So determine exactly whom you want to reach. Then tie in what you want with the desires and interests of the persons you are trying to influence. But you may ask, "Can I be sure of reaching every member of a specific audience?" No, not exactly; but if you know your audience well enough, you can determine the average approach. In turn, this procedure gives you the chance to catch and hold interest—and cause the desired response—of the majority of your public.

You can't catalogue appeals like so many vitamins. Each one is unique to a certain situation. No matter what your approach, you must give it the acid test by asking the question, "How important is my approach to the people I am trying to influence?"

How can you tune your public relations program to the right key? First of all, you must assume that people may not be remotely interested in your objectives. That is an extreme view, but by starting from there, you can proceed from the known to the unknown. Remember, the public doesn't know as much about your objectives as you do. If it did, there would be little need for strong public relations programs.

Use the following check list for increased harmony:
1. How does the public feel toward the idea?
Now you won't get this information by guessing. Facts and opinions will come from surveys, conversations, panel discussions, local editorials, and many other sources. By knowing the general climate of opinion, you can plan your ideas so that they can be channeled at a certain level.

School officials in Middletown, for instance, want a new school gymnasium. Everyone in town, from the old folks to the small fry, is sports-minded. In a situation like this, the school officials have no great problem. Not many miles away, however, school officials at Blankville also want a new gymnasium. A few crusty tightwads, who think sports and physical education are just so many "fads and frills," are the molders of public opinion. Here the superintendent has a real problem in convincing the community that it needs a gymnasium.

2. How much does the specific public know about the plan, idea, or objective?

Are most of your citizens already familiar with "parents' night," for example? Or is it a new program, something which has never been presented in the community before? School officials in a city in Missouri were criticized recently because they sponsored a three-day workshop for teachers (all schools were dismissed) in October. What was wrong? No one had bothered to explain to the citizens the purposes and benefits—to both teachers and pupils—of such an undertaking. The more revolutionary your idea, the more time you must devote to explaining it so that it will be accepted.

3. Does this idea, event, or proposal have any unique feature or advantage?

Most communities will support programs which they consider up to date and workable. They don't want to be known as backward. They want to keep in step with other progressive communities. Knowing this, the superintendent should always think in terms of benefits, advantages, and positive results when intepreting his ideas. A word of warning: Do not endow your idea with advantages which do not exist except in your imagination.

4. Make it easy for people to respond.

Today it is not enough merely to convince people of the desirability of doing a certain thing. You must lure them from their other interests into an eager willingness to help the schools. How can this be done? Suggest to the P.T.A. president that a transportation committee be set up. Tell the public—by direct mail, advertisements of local merchants, news stories, and other means—that an architect's drawing of the new high school building may be seen in the window of the electric light and power company.

"Attend openhouse at the school in your neighborhood Tuesday night" is meaningless if the person reading the announcement in the newspaper doesn't have any idea where the school nearest him is located. "Oh, but the children will tell their parents and other relatives," you say. Yes, most of them will, but what about the new citizens, the couples without children, elderly persons, and others who may attend? Do everything within your power to make it easy for people to respond to your request.

5. Does your idea, plan, or objective compete with local interests?

In a sense, every school event is competitive from the standpoint of time, financial support, leadership, and other factors. For example, many schools in small communities never schedule events on Wednesday night because they would conflict with midweek church services. It isn't enough that an educational cause be different from other community causes. Rather, the school head must present it in such a way that the difference must be of definite plus-value to those he is trying to persuade. Look for exclusive features, advantages, or benefits, and then tie them in with what the citizens are seeking.

6. Co-operative planning means wider acceptance.

It is much easier for a superintendent to know at what level to project his program if parents have worked with him in its formation, for then he has already secured a group of boosters who are enthusiastic and fully educated. They can give the campaign a big push in its beginning. And, too, laymen usually exert more influence on other laymen than do school representatives. Thus it is easy enough for the school head to have a certain degree of favorable public opinion on his side when he launches any project.

What is the main factor? It is just this: Establish a common meeting ground for you and your public. The foundation for your plan must be laid in the realm of what your prospect already knows. In this way, you win his confidence through your agreement with him on facts he already believes. Do this successfully, and your program will be tuned to the right key.

6. *Ethics Come First*

SUCCESSFUL PUBLIC RELATIONS are built on research, knowledge of public attitudes, awareness of the best uses for various media, and other elements; but without ethics the program cannot survive. Honesty is the law of public opinion and must always be obeyed.

What are the basic requirements? Rex F. Harlow says, "Public relations activities must be honest, truthful, open, authoritative, and responsible; they must be fair and realistic; and they must be conducted in the public interest."

School leaders need not worry about an elaborate code. Rather, they must seek to be truthful and fair in all their relationships and contacts. In short, they must seek to keep all activities on the plane of life's greatest principle of behavior—the Golden Rule. Modern life is now so complex that anything but openness in the conduct of an institution is self-defeating. If the superintendent reacts with an it's-none-of-their-business attitude when the public asks questions, his schools will suffer in public confidence, and people will regard him with suspicion.

By the very nature of school public relations, the activities and results are on display for the critical examination of the public. It is hard to find a public relations program today which does not invite and urge citizens to visit schools, inspect them, and watch them in action. Because of this, administrators must be more careful than ever that they are accurate, fair, and factual in their interpretative efforts. Any misrepresentation means that an opportunity to tell the truth has been lost. The result of such unwise practice will be public censure. "I never misrepresent any phase of my program," a superintendent may declare. To be sure, he may be perfectly sincere in making that statement. But is he mistaken in his belief? Can he support his point of view with facts? His information must be accurate, no matter what the cost.

Lack of authority hinders many school public relations pro-

24

grams. Provision should be made by the superintendent that all official contacts made by principals, assistant superintendents, teachers, the director of public relations, and others, are fully authorized. School personnel must realize that they have responsibilities both to the system and to the supporting public. The person who is unwilling to stand solidly behind what he says and does is not worthy of public trust. Statements of officials and workers must be dependable and supported by facts. Those who interpret any phase of the educational program to the public must bear the stamp of responsibility. Then, and only then, will the system earn the reputation for making good all its promises and representations.

To illustrate: Miss X, the principal of Longfellow School, is called by a reporter who wants to know the details of how Susie Jones fell from a slide and broke her arm. Miss X says, "I'm sorry, but I can't give you that information." The reporter fumes and calls the superintendent. The superintendent calls Miss X. Two hours later the reporter obtains the essential facts. The result: poor press relations for the system. How easy it would have been for Miss X, aware of her responsibility as principal, to have given the reporter the information. She should know both her limitations and her obligations in all public contacts. Most important, she should know public relations policies well enough to talk and act freely within the framework of the general program.

Truth and fairness always pay. If the superintendent is a clever operator, he may fool part of the people part of the time, but this won't be continued indefinitely. The typical superintendent does not work in privacy. Just about everything he does is sooner or later exposed to public view.

School administrators must be completely frank in their relationships with the public. That is the belief of W. T. White, former president of the American Association of School Administrators and superintendent of schools at Dallas, Texas. He declares, "It is shortsighted and contributes to suspicion and lack of confidence to follow any other policy.

"For example, a community may be projecting and carrying

on a building program. Perhaps the taxpayers and those who are responsible for the over-all financial condition of the community feel that it is desirable for the sake of the credit of the community to ask bond authorizations in two installments of smaller denominations, rather than to have one issue of a much larger denomination. In such case the school administration should be perfectly honest with the public. The administration should tell the public that the first issue is only a partial fulfillment of the needs, and should explain how the credit of the community is involved and reasons which may be valid for asking for only a part of the needed funds; then, furthermore, the administration should tell the community that within the specified length of time an additional authorization for borrowing will be requested of the community." Honesty in dealing with the public will bring untold rewards.

Education and educational institutions are not products to be sold. They are constantly being revised and adapted to meet new needs as a co-operative project of the American people. Participation of citizens in this task is not accomplished at the suggestion of the director of public relations. Belmont Farley, director of press and radio relations of the National Education Association, observes that this action "is prescribed by law. The people represent themselves by legal action on his board of directors, and approve or disapprove at the ballot box any extensive change in school services. This is inherent in the nature of a public enterprise." For these reasons, the ethical considerations in educational public relations are unique.

"Shall we withhold some of the facts?" is a question which arises frequently in any strategy to influence the public. Company scientists might know the shortcomings of their product. This would be a company secret. At least the information would not travel beyond the conferences of executives, sales managers, and experts. Such a policy on the part of educational leaders, however, would be fatal. After all, the schools belong to the people. They are entitled to know the truth.

There is no price tag on the esteem of the community. It must be merited and won on the basis of sound educational policies and actions which will withstand the acid test of public scrutiny. Any school system which bases its public relations program on an honest, ethical foundation will gain public acceptance.

7. *Before You Make the Budget*

IT IS WELL TO REMEMBER that the success or failure of a public relations program can never be measured in terms of its budget. Some of the smallest schools, with limited expenditures for strengthening good will, have developed highly successful programs.

How can public relations expenditures be determined? No really satisfactory method can be outlined in detail because of the variables and intangibles involved. And, too, the objectives must always be considered.

Here are some general suggestions to keep in mind:

1. Define clearly the size and scope of the over-all program planned by school officials.

2. Know where and how public relations can be a factor in achieving the objectives.

3. Select carefully the various media and channels to be used.

4. Know the attitudes of the persons and publics to be reached.

5. Consider expenditure of funds in the light of a lasting, consistent program rather than a temporary one.

6. Set up a budget which will be in proportion to the total revenue of the system, and see that once the budget is approved it is not trimmed with every passing wind.

7. Accord public relations a top place in the administrative program, not only in normal times and boom periods, but in depressions as well.

8. Weigh each procedure in public relations with current and future requirements in mind.

9. Remember that the success of a program is largely depend-

ent on the spirit of all groups within the system, not on the amount spent for public relations.

10. Provide means for financing special needs which may arise from time to time.

11. See that the budget of the public relations program— which is the "voice" of the system—is not the first item to be reduced when economy is sought.

12. Know in advance the extent to which proposed ideas are already established in the mind of the public. The only way to get the facts called for by this problem is through research.

13. Determine the size of your public. How many persons should be reached? Can a mass appeal be used or must the basic ideas be broken down into various appeals?

14. Remember that the best budget is built when all the facts have been assembled, reviewed, and weighed—a slow, painstaking process.

Intensive study and research must precede any budget estimate. Get all the facts and opinions you can from all sources. Reports of home visitation, records of past campaigns, editorial clippings, ways in which all media and channels (from a speakers' bureau to pamphlets taken home by children) have been used in the past, responses to radio broadcasts, the reaction of the public, either as groups or individuals, to past appeals— these are but a few of the sources which should be studied.

Even though the superintendent examines past practices and results, he cannot rely on this information alone in planning his new budget. He must collect all material worth interpreting, and at the same time he must examine the nature of the task that lies ahead. When he has done this, he can select the most promising methods of reaching his goals. "Each year's campaign involves a task which is new in some respect," a wise superintendent has stated. "Old measurements and old answers, accepted uncritically, are not good enough."

Most public relations strategies must be planned in advance. If this is not done, the program will lack continuity and momentum. More important, any approach which builds public acceptance is not likely to come to the superintendent on the spur of the moment. Usually, it is the result of planning sessions, conferences, committee meetings—in short, work, and plenty of it.

An ever present factor in determining the amount to be spent for public relations is the general economic condition of the community. When business is off, each dollar spent for public relations must carry a greater load than normally. Let us remember this: It is unwise economy to cut public relations budgets during depression periods. This is the very time when the public should be reminded of the potential worth of education.

"How much shall we spend on public relations?" That is the question facing scores of superintendents. We must realize first of all that many phases of the program require no expenditure of money; but they do require the time and abilities of many persons. Second, it is well to remember that whatever amount is spent is justified, provided it is used for well-planned activities. Enough money must be assured to provide a continuing program—one which makes positive contacts with many individuals and many groups from day to day. The important thing for you to know is the public attitude toward your system. Then you can determine the approximate budget needed to reach the desired goals.

8. *Leadership Starts at the Top*

IF ANYONE NEEDS a multiple personality, it is the superintendent of schools. His public expects him to be a financial wizard, author, speaker, scholar, politician, diplomat, adviser to the school board, active civic worker, administrator, and public relations counselor of the highest rank. The strains and worries of his office are many, but his position is rich in opportunities for achievement.

Duties and obligations of the office have expanded to a tremendous degree. When the office was first instituted in 1837, the superintendent's role was almost exclusively that of routine administration of the schools. Today the superintendent's opportunities for leadership are much greater. On him and his colleagues everywhere rests the task not only of increasing the nation's educational facilities to take care of the expanded needs which the future will bring, but also of remedying many serious deficiencies which exist today. Above all, he must act as co-ordinator of school and community efforts to solve problems common to both and to set goals for both to attain. As the chief representative of education in his community, he has a unique opportunity to influence the educational thinking of its citizens.

Communication between the superintendent and the public is always a two-way process. "A school superintendent should make it his business to inform his community about every phase of school operations," it is noted by William A. Early, superintendent of schools, Arlington County, Virginia. "But," he warns, "public relations should not stop there. The superintendent should not only give out information; he should also learn what the people are thinking about the schools and other community enterprises."

A successful superintendent must be democratic in all of his activities. He must consider the opinions and interests of the whole community in planning the educational program. He cannot confine his attention to a small group of the "right people," as is sometimes done.

Merely working hard at his job isn't enough. In addition, he must avoid practices which may arouse hostility or contempt on the part of his public. He cannot evade the responsibilities of leadership. If he does, apathy toward the schools and their needs will result. He is automatically the most important worker in the school public relations program. What can he do to strengthen his leadership?

School public relations cannot be a one-man affair. For this reason, the superintendent must organize and direct his program in such a way that the entire school personnel takes part in planning and executing all phases of public contacts. Actually, the over-all program may rise or fall on his ability to organize a co-operative effort.

The splendid booklet, *Community Leadership,* published by

the American Association of School Administrators, states that the role of the superintendent of schools is twofold: he must fire people with enthusiasm to do something about improving their schools, and he must release the energies of community life that will enable people to develop the kinds of schools they need and want.

The alert superintendent must take advantage of every possible opportunity to improve his knowledge of public relations. He may receive guidance and information from (1) literature, (2) workshops, (3) other school systems, (4) courses in residence at a college or university, (5) interviews with competent public relations experts, (6) attendance at state, regional, and national gatherings, and (7) personnel of his own system.

Regardless of the number of other professional groups which beckon, the superintendent should become a member of the National School Public Relations Association. This organization is one of the departments of the National Education Association and has a membership of more than 2,200 educators, including public relations personnel, superintendents, principals, teachers, board members, and association leaders. Two of its many services are the publications *Trends,* a monthly newsletter, and *Techniques,* a series of "how-to-do-it" leaflets prepared by experts.

The superintendent of schools is a 'social engineer," it is observed by George D. Strayer, professor emeritus of Teachers College, Columbia University. "He must enjoy the confidence and good will of the board of education. One of his major responsibilities is to help community leaders understand the significance of the school program. In larger systems the superintendent is supported by a highly specialized staff, but in no case can he delegate to another his duty of interpreting the educational program to the public."

Most important of all, the superintendent must develop public relations consciousness. Now this doesn't necessarily come from reading magazine articles or listening to lectures. Rather, he develops this vital ability by thinking of every act, every influence, every situation—even an event which may occur at some future time—in the light of its significance to his public relations program. When he develops this ability, he can put in motion the processes and techniques necessary to command and sustain public acceptance. He learns what the public thinks of the schools; he suggests ways of building good will; and he designs policies which will establish leadership for the system.

Andrew D. Holt, former president of the National Education Association, now administrative assistant to the president of the University of Tennessee, believes that a superintendent must set the example for his teachers. "Whether we like it or not, the superintendent's professional attitude is usually reflected in the attitude of his teachers. If he affiliates with his professional organizations, attends their meetings, and participates in their activities, his teachers will usually do likewise. If he refuses to spend his hard-earned money for association dues, goes fishing on convention days, and looks down his nose at the activities of his professional organizations, his teachers will generally follow suit."

Whatever the local situation, the superintendent fits his personality to his particular community. Let us suppose that Superintendent J writes effectively. Then he should capitalize on that talent. Perhaps another school leader has the ability to work with community groups, but is not effective as a public speaker. Then he should concentrate on group work, and let others make the speeches. Each one must make the most of his abilities and recognize his shortcomings. He must consider his total impact as an individual.

How far can the superintendent project his leadership without incurring the resentment of co-workers and patrons? His picture should not be used in every brochure issued by the system. He need not be quoted in every news item. Nor should he always ride in the first automobile in the high school homecoming parade. There are times when he must perform certain duties as superintendent, but on many occasions he can see to it that his associates and teachers assume active roles as public relations agents. He should exercise care that his personal leadership is balanced.

By virtue of his position, the superintendent is the executive head of the public relations program. He furnishes creative leadership, directs the formation of policies, advises workers, and establishes procedures. He points out what should be done in public relations objectives, suggests means for accomplishing those goals, stimulates interest in the program, and then delegates the details to responsible associates. He keeps in touch with personnel, parents, and others through interviews, bulletins, reports, letters, and conferences.

He may appoint a committee on public relations, with the authority to (1) initiate its own investigations and report directly to him on matters of institutional concern, (2) consider problems referred to it by the superintendent, (3) analyze public relations problems and procedures, and (4) adapt ideas from other systems.

The superintendent must have a sympathetic ear for public relations problems and set aside time to consider them. He must have faith and confidence in those delegated to carry out specific functions and show a certain tolerance toward diversity in point of view.

As chief representative of the public school system, the superintendent must

1. be fair and considerate;
2. be approachable, accessible, and helpful to others;
3. be consistent, sincere, responsible, and decisive;
4. use authority democratically and wisely;
5. have the courage to stand behind a principle;
6. be of superior intellectual capacity;
7. possess sound judgment, common sense, and emotional stability;
8. have a good sense of humor;
9. have a high degree of social intelligence;
10. have the drive necessary to work hard and persistently;
11. know the secret of getting the co-operation of others;
12. seek always to improve himself and his system;

13. set an example for his workers in conduct, methods, and goals;

14. have an abiding faith in the importance of education;

15. above all, be an expert in human relations.

In order to insure successful relations with staff and public, the superintendent must

1. recognize the potentialities—good and bad—of public relations;

2. develop complete harmony within the school system;

3. know his staff and teachers as individuals;

4. encourage people to make suggestions;

5. take his workers into his confidence;

6. use tact and diplomacy in his criticisms and suggestions;

7. give praise to those to whom it is due;

8. analyze the work of the staff as a whole to discover its strength and weakness;

9. report frequently to the staff, to the board, and to the community on conditions within the system;

10. train a good public relations assistant, in order that the program never lacks a leader;

11. bring before the people the information necessary for an understanding of the nature of the schools' needs and problems;

12. maintain high standards in the system;

13. lead in the development of policies;

14. take an active role in community planning;

15. provide services which are essential in operating the education program.

As the key person in the public relations program, the superintendent must bear a large share of the burden in creating a solid backlog of public understanding. He must build confidence not only in the personnel of his system, but throughout the whole sphere of community relationships. Ultimately, neglect or indifference on the part of the superintendent will seriously affect every phase of the relations between school and public.

9. *Principals: Second in Command*

ONE PROMINENT CITY SUPERINTENDENT, who has been more than successful in gaining public favor for his system, summed up the principal's role in education in this way: "The principal is the administrative field officer of public education."

Just as his immediate superior has certain duties to perform, he too has definite public relations responsibilities—not in the same groups, perhaps, nor on the same large scale, but he can make positive contacts in many areas. He can make his school the focal point of neighborhood activities. As the leader of a group of teachers, he must keep his staff alert to their public relations possibilities.

"Joiner" though he would like to be, the principal cannot spread himself too thin among various community groups. Unless he is careful, he may find that outside demands have grown so great that his duties at school are often neglected. He must analyze his particular situation and then decide to what lay groups he can give his time and abilities. As principal, he is the public relations leader in the area in which his school is located.

What are the needs of the community? What are its resources? Answers to these questions will not come easily. But the principal must know some of the answers if the school is to contribute, immediately or ultimately, to the improvement of the community. Public support will come only in proportion to the public's understanding of what the schools are doing and why. The principal must

1. possess common sense, judgment, discretion, and a sense of proportion.
2. be able to express himself clearly in speech and writing.
3. be tactful and diplomatic in all his relationships.
4. be liked by students attending his school.
5. be able to "grin and bear it" when things go wrong.
6. be a leader, both in the school and in the community.
7. be approachable by teachers, parents, and all others.

35

8. know his staff members as individuals.

9. have organizing ability in order to make the most of his personnel and situation.

10. keep his staff working smoothly and harmoniously.

11. welcome new ideas and suggestions.

12. know how to solve social conflicts between teachers and students, teachers and parents, and how to reduce professional tension which may exist among his group of teachers.

13. carry out the plans of the superintendent and school board.

14. keep the superintendent informed of any situation which may later become a problem in public relations.

15. make it a point to know as many parents in the area served by his school as possible, and encourage his teachers to do the same.

16. know public thought in his district.

17. work closely with community groups which function in his area.

18. stress the importance of strengthening public relations by means of staff meetings, visual aids, special literature, letters, bulletins, and other channels.

19. be public relations conscious in everything he does.

As an active agent in the public relations program, the principal faces many problems. By staying in close touch with patrons and other citizens of his neighborhood, he will know their attitudes toward his school and toward education in general. He must be sensitive to the public mind. Yet no matter how community-minded he may be, he must be alert to his school and its activities. He must keep up to date professionally —not only in educational procedures, but in public relations techniques as well—by reading current professional literature, attending conferences and short courses, corresponding with others in similar situations, taking part in workshops, and being genuinely interested in his job. The most important thing to remember is that public relations activities are not to be reserved for special occasions, but must function in normal day-to-day relationships.

10. *The Teacher's Role*

PUBLIC REGARD for schools can never reach a higher level than that of those who teach. Here is the front line of public relations. Day after day, hour after hour, the teachers are making impressions which carry a terrific impact into community life. Someone once said, "As the child thinks of the teacher, so the home thinks of the school."

Too often the teacher confines his human relations to the classroom. Frequently he holds himself aloof from the community, its organizations, and its leaders. In too many instances, his only acquaintances are other members of the faculty. Such teachers should not be surprised that the public fails to appreciate them and to understand their problems.

How can a teacher increase the community's respect for himself and his profession? First, he should get out of the classroom and meet people, not only as a teacher but as an individual. Second, teachers must stop being so apologetic about their profession. If they hold a high opinion of their work, others will feel that it is worthy. Third, the teacher must understand that education is a co-operative endeavor and that public relations are strengthened when all individuals and groups concerned work as a team.

The teacher must realize that he is very important in the public relations program. He must see that by doing an effective teaching job he is making a notable contribution to public understanding and support. Like the superintendent and the principal, he should realize that every situation will have some effect on the public's conception of the school. If he has had little training in public relations, he should read current literature on the subject.

Every teacher should recognize the value of tact, courtesy, and friendliness toward all with whom he comes in contact. He must remember that to all of those he meets—both in and out of school—he is the school system.

The teacher should be active in community life. In a city or town of any size he should take part in the representative interests of the citizens. The effective teacher is a vital person. He goes places and does things. He impresses others, particularly children, as being positive and alive.

The teacher should be a reporting agent. Often he can warn the principal or superintendent of an impending crisis. Of course, he must first be made to feel that his reports and suggestions are welcomed by his administrator. Above all, the teacher must use discretion in talking about school matters to friends outside the system.

When is a teacher overworked? Obviously, the situation is the answer. If Miss Lucile Doubleday has a class of sixty-four students seven hours a day, her teaching cannot be very effective. Nor can she be expected to do a great deal of extra work in public relations.

"But," you say, "a few teachers do all the work." That is true in many situations. Just because Mr. Harvey P. Gogetter is able and willing is no reason why he should be overburdened either in the classroom or out. Every principal should see that his faculty load is fair and equitable.

Teachers cannot do their best work if they are weighed down with clerical tasks. Too many reports, too many records, and too many surveys usually result in fatigue rather than facts. Some paper work is necessary. But the same amount of time could be spent more profitably in contacts with students and parents.

Because teachers are key individuals in the public relations program, they should become acquainted with as many parents as their limited time permits. They should not feel that their visits are perfunctory duty calls, but that they are a basis for friendly understanding and collaboration.

Like any professional worker, the teacher must keep growing. He should be assertive in local groups who are working to improve school conditions. He should spend some time in advanced study or travel, or work in some other field during the summer. In so doing, he will broaden his horizons.

The effective teacher believes that his job is an important one, and he expects others to think so as well. He gives evidence that he has special skill and knowledge. He treats other teachers and staff members—regardless of their titles, positions, or salaries—as professional equals and valued co-workers.

In this manner do teachers work on the front line of public relations. If they bear in mind their tremendous influence on the life of the community and constantly strive to make that influence a positive one, they will help to build public understanding and good will.

11. *Public Relations Begin at Home*   VIP

NOT MANY YEARS AGO the superintendent performed great and mighty deeds in public relations. All of a sudden, he awoke to the realization that he wasn't the only worker in building good will and understanding. To be sure, he considered teachers as part of the public relations program, at least in times of crisis. He may have suggested a few activities to members of the school board. But in most instances, he ignored the possibilities of utilizing clerks, custodians, secretaries, nurses, cafeteria managers, school doctors, and many other employees as active public relations agents.

The gruff bus driver, the impertinent secretary, and the unkempt custodian create negative impressions. Humanly enough, a person who has been treated discourteously by any employee is likely to believe that all personnel of the system are tactless and indifferent.

School personnel in all their varied duties and tasks constitute one of the most valuable and easily cultivated groups in the whole system. Evidence is accumulating that the wise superintendent is doing everything possible to educate all helpers to their public relations responsibilities.

Twin Oaks School may not have much of a problem. Superintendent H knows teachers, custodians, and bus drivers by their first names. He knows their families, their hobbies, and takes an interest in them as individuals. Naturally, they know as much about him and his methods. But as the system begins to grow, especially when new buildings and new staffs continue to be added, the personal contact between superintendent and personnel becomes increasingly difficult and finally almost impossible. Then the system is confronted by the problem of what to do to retain or recapture the "family" spirit.

Personnel must be reminded that they are more than their titles indicate. Furthermore, the superintendent must explain to them their tremendous roles as active agents in gaining public favor. Every contact, no matter how trivial it may seem to the employee, is an opportunity to promote good will. "I don't expect all personnel to understand everything about our program even though I try to keep them informed through many channels," a superintendent remarked. "I do, however, expect them to be courteous, tactful, friendly, and as well informed as possible."

One thing is certain: No superintendent can afford to allow his personnel to learn public relations principles and duties by chance. People must be told of their responsibilities, and they must be reminded of them regularly. On occasions, the leader must do some follow-up work to see that suggestions have been put into action.

Each worker must realize that his work is a vital factor in the total impact of the schools on public thought. One of the best means of emphasizing this thought is the employees' manual. Here is a suggested statement which a superintendent might use:

YOU are most important to your co-workers. What you do and what you do not do directly affects them. You are a member of a big team that wants to win. You have a definite place on that team as do the other members, from the highest paid to the lowest paid. What you do meshes with what they are doing and smooth meshing is what makes the wheels turn and the machine tick. YOU are vital to the rest just as the rest are vital to you, so be proud of the job that is yours and hold its standards high.

As YOU are judged by your co-workers during the working hours, so shall you be judged by those with whom you come into contact during your hours away from your school. The impression you make as a member of various organizations—fraternal, civic, religious, recreational—in short, everything you do influences the opinions of others. Therefore, it is just as important that you be a good citizen and a good neighbor as it is that you be a conscientious worker.

So far as the people of Blankville are concerned, the public school system is not a remote and mysterious operation—it is the school employees they chance to meet. Actually, your public consists of your personal friends and the people you meet as you do your job. To them, on the other hand, you are the school system. Through your friends and all persons with whom you come in contact, the school system will grow and be understood. Yes, it is as simple as that.

In the final analysis, public relations comes down to this: If you are informed, pleasant, and co-operative, and if you act in a manner to command respect, you are doing all that can be asked of you by the system. In addition, you are doing yourself an excellent service, both as an employee and as a citizen, for such behavior means success—in every sense of that important word.

Welcome to our "family." May your new association bring you the best of everything.

As an example
Secretaries occupy key positions in the schools' contacts with the public. Each one should realize that her duties, many and varied, offer countless opportunities to create understanding for the educational system. She must be tactful, a good listener, and friendly to all. Ability to remember names and faces will strengthen her influence. Sometimes she must protect the superintendent or principal from unnecessary interviews. On

41

many occasions she must direct a person to other offices or schools and at the same time leave the caller satisfied with his brief visit. She should see that each visitor receives courteous attention.

Like other persons engaged in nonteaching duties, the secretary must remember that she is the first, and often the only, person with whom parents and other visitors make contact. She should be well informed. "How many teachers were in the system in 1938?" someone asks over the telephone. She answers that question only to find a gentleman standing in front of her desk, who asks "Could you tell me who is making out the city P.T.A. calendar for next year?" Luckily, she knows the answer to that question. Others aren't so easy.

If some disgruntled person wants to "unload" on the superintendent, he may tell all his troubles to the secretary. At times, she may have to listen to persons who have had unpleasant experiences with the schools and their personnel. Whatever the situation, she must be tactful, understanding, patient, and courteous.

Is your custodian a help or a handicap? He should play an influential role in the public relations setup. Because of his many contacts with teachers, students, parents, and the public, his actions and attitudes are far-reaching. N. L. George, business manager of the Oklahoma City public schools, holds a two-day short course for custodians and other building service employees each year in August. His suggestions follow:

1. The custodian is responsible to the superintendent of schools, the principal of the building in which he works, the director of business, the head building custodian, and the head supervising custodian.

2. The custodian must be courteous, friendly, and helpful. He must show respect for others if he expects others to treat him with respect. He must remain quiet and keep his temper when people are rude and unkind. (Of course, there are limits to everything, and he has a perfect right to protest against unreasonable requests and abuse.)

3. In his relations with the principal, he must respect and carry out rules and regulations. He should feel free to discuss frankly any differences in opinion, and he should remember that in a sense he is the principal's right-hand man. Furthermore, he should recognize that the principal knows the importance of a good custodian and is well aware that a clean, well-kept, and properly heated and ventilated building influences favorably the teaching of the instructors and the learning of the children.

4. In his relations with the teachers, he should be courteous, friendly, and obliging, and should try to help them in a cheerful and pleasant manner, without grumbling or attempting to excuse himself from additional duties they may request. He should always go to the principal if there is a misunderstanding, rather than lose his temper or argue loudly with the teacher—especially before pupils. He should always consult the teacher before entering a classroom during recitation or study periods. Then he should enter quietly and perform his job with as little disturbance as possible.

5. In his relations with pupils, the custodian should be pleasant, friendly, and patient. When the need comes to direct or correct them, he should do it in a quiet and respectful manner. He can set them an ideal example of gentlemanly conduct.

6. In his relations with the general public, he should be courteous and helpful to all who visit his building. He should use common sense and discretion in talking about school matters to his friends.

To sum it up, the custodian can build favorable opinion for the schools by being courteous, obliging, friendly, patient, loyal to his associates, and reliable.

Example

Few schools realize the importance of bus drivers in the total public relations picture. Qualifications for drivers include (1) good personal habits, (2) reliability, (3) promptness, (4) competency, (5) physical fitness, (6) neatness, (7) first-aid knowledge, (8) a pleasant attitude, (9) a record of safe driving, and (10) the ability to maintain a high standard of student conduct.

Just as important, the drivers should be reminded of their duties in public relations. The wise administrator will use motion pictures, slides, film strips, and other visual aids to stress courtesy, kindness, fairness, and other desirable characteristics. Meetings should be held periodically for the discussion of common problems.

No matter what the scope of the in-service program, its studies and activities must be directed by the superintendent. Of course, he may assign the details to the principal or a committee; but he is responsible for its success or failure. His leadership and constant support are needed in this vital phase of the program.

As in any co-operative group effort, a successful employee public relations program will depend on two factors: each worker's knowledge of his duties, responsibilities, opportunities, and limitations, and the extent of his loyalty and interest in the well-being of his school system.

12. *Yardsticks to Measure Personnel*

IT IS QUITE OBVIOUS that not all personnel in any school system will do an equally good job in public relations. Every staff has its star performers and its failures. And today, when there are so many misconceptions regarding education, few systems can afford a high percentage of employees whose efforts show on the negative side of the ledger.

It is wise to measure the effectiveness of your personnel at regular intervals. These checkups will help you to (1) discover those employees whose work is bringing good will, (2) to spot the staff members who may need help, and (3) to find ways of strengthening the over-all program.

Here are some guideposts for measuring performance:

1. Does each person understand his responsibilities and his limitations as a public relations agent?

2. Do you specify the exact duties of your personnel?

44

3. Do your employees understand that their public relations duties may vary, depending upon the time and place? For example, does the teacher know how much authority he has when he is away from school?

4. Do certain staff members make the same mistakes in their contacts from time to time?

5. Do you ever thank or reward workers who contribute a "plus" to their work and thus build understanding and harmony for the system?

6. Do you require all personnel to submit periodic reports showing their publications, membership on committees, honors and awards, election to office, number of home visitations, membership in community organizations, and other activities?

7. Do you keep in close touch with staff members who are emotionally unstable? The person who loses his temper, who is overly sensitive, or who fancies himself slighted is a poor risk in the profession and is certainly a weak link in the public relations chain.

8. Do you encourage employees who use their imaginations constructively? They are alert and progressive, and are the best sources for ideas in improving your program.

9. Do you set a good example for your personnel? A school system is no more dynamic than its superintendent and principals.

10. Ask for action! When you have outlined your program and explained the duties of each person, get the staff members to do something about it.

11. How do your staff members spend their vacations—traveling, studying, working, writing? The ambitious person, one who is on his way up, is a great asset.

12. Remember—consider each employee from the standpoint of the total impression he makes. If he is positive and constructive, give him an "A" for his performance.

STEPS IN STRENGTHENING STAFF RELATIONS

Your staff members—teachers and service employees—are your representatives. You have the task of keeping them happy. In addition, you must train them so that they will make every contact count:

1. Explain and interpret policies, so that misunderstandings will not occur.

2. Seek to maintain a constant high level of interest and morale.

3. Determine your staff members' skills and capacities.

4. Delegate duties with the interests of the various employees in mind.

5. Determine the qualities of leadership of each staff member.

6. Hold group discussions on ways of improving the program.

7. Distribute informative bulletins on procedures and topics at hand.

8. Use films and handbooks as training aids.

9. Encourage staff members to offer suggestions.

10. Emphasize the importance of their role as reporting agents.

11. See that each employee knows the tested techniques of human relations.

12. Emphasize the need for sound planning, logical thinking, clear writing, and effective speaking.

13. Be tactful in supervision.

14. Learn what is causing nonco-operative attitudes.

15. Remember that staff education is a continuing process.

Employee relations can be improved through the use of:

1. Opinion polls. These provide a two-way means of communication. In addition, they invite frank expression of policies, procedures, and so on. Never take a poll and then keep the findings a secret. Always issue a report to staff members on the results. Strengthen the program by using as many of the sug-

46

gestions as possible, and explain why certain recommended changes cannot be made at present.

2. Letters. These establish a personal contact which helps to build good will. Letters may be written in commendation for fine work or a new idea, congratulations on a special occasion, or condolence or sympathy.

3. Staff reports. An informed personnel is of vital importance in a school system. In some instances, the annual report of the superintendent is sent to all employees. If this is not done, it is well to issue a brief report exclusively for employees. In an ideal situation, each staff member should get a copy of every bulletin, report, or pamphlet which is issued from the superintendent's office.

4. Inspection trips. The wise superintendent will make plans for his employees to visit school systems of other cities. He will see that his custodians attend the refresher short course at a near-by college. In every instance, he will do all that he can to encourage teachers and others to keep abreast of the newest trends and developments in their respective fields.

5. Publicity stories. At all times the superintendent should give recognition to outstanding achievements of teachers and staff members. He may do this through stories in school publications, the local press, and other media. In addition, he can mention them in his speeches and in casual conversation. At all times he should seek to enhance the prestige of his co-workers. Increased understanding and support necessarily require public acceptance of the worth of the entire school personnel.

6. Training literature. Readership is high in training manuals, employee handbooks, and similar publications. For the most part, the person who reads them wants to improve his efficiency. To make training literature effective, be sure that it has an attractive layout and illustrations which clarify the text.

Encourage teamwork and loyalty by means of an employee handbook. Properly planned, an employee manual can be invaluable in molding teachers, principals, and members of the nonteaching staff into a cohesive working unit. It will give an

47

employee a sense of security, and will make him contented, loyal, and helpful.

Since the handbook deals with human emotions and motivations, it should be prepared with care. A handbook of rules alone, for example, would do more harm than good. A personal letter of welcome from the superintendent to "YOU" will set the desired tone of friendliness and informality. The copy should be written from the point of view of the employee's interest and should be clear and easily understood.

Here are some topics which may be discussed:

brief historical sketch of system

divisions and departments

directory of buildings and principal offices

directory of officers and members of the school board

school publications, reports, and newsletters

general policies

retirement program

employee benefits and privileges

insurance program

service awards

physical examination

safety

first aid, medical facilities

pay checks

training programs

hours

holidays

sick leave

lunch and rest periods

recreation program

library

use of special equipment

ordering supplies

parking lots

bulletin boards

publicity

clothing

personal mail

telephone calls

smoking

soliciting

public relations responsibilities

The use of illustrations will fix important details in the mind of the employee so that he will remember them rapidly. Strive for simplicity in art and layout. An employee handbook is one of the cornerstones of your program. It is an investment, not an expense.

What superintendent hasn't said to himself, "How I wish that I had some new public relations ideas!" He knows that his program must be interesting, that variety must be injected from time to time, and that new strategies must be used.

Has he ever asked for suggestions from staff members? It isn't likely; but if he has, he knows the value of a suggestion system. Of course, employees will submit all kinds of ideas. Some will be of no value, but usually quite a number of practical, useful ideas will emerge.

Some of the suggestions will appear in the form of observations or comments. They should point out a specific need and the reason for it. "Lights should be installed on the parking lot," recommended one teacher. Where did she get this idea? Several patrons had told her that they would attend more night meetings of the P.T.A. if they didn't have to park their cars on a darkened lot.

Many ideas are simple and easy to put into operation. "Let's use student reception committees, stationed near the entrances, on 'parents' night,'" a teacher suggested. The idea was followed, and it proved to be an excellent builder of good will.

Employees should be rewarded for their ideas. Commercial firms give cash prizes, but, of course, that procedure cannot be followed in the schools. One system presents certificates to staff members whose suggestions are considered worth while by the central committee, and the winners are introduced by the superintendent at the annual dinner.

Suggestion systems often fail to accomplish their purpose because (1) publicity regarding the program has not been effectively planned, (2) the superintendent, principals, and school board members fail to give support to the project, (3) recognition is not in keeping with the value of the suggestions, (4) staff members have not been convinced of the merit of the program, or (5) no definite authority has been delegated for carrying out the program.

Membership on the award board should be representative of all groups serving the system, both academic and nonacademic. Principals, supervisors, and heads of other groups should

49

urge that each staff member submit a number of suggestions. Every proposal should be acknowledged as soon as possible after it is received by the board. If the idea cannot be used, the employee should be told the reason for its rejection, thanked for his response, and urged to try again.

Thorough publicity is necessary in getting a big response. Letters from the superintendent, stories in the employee handbook, posters for bulletin boards, and news items in the staff newspaper may all be used to keep workers informed and interested. Announcement of the winners should be publicized in the same manner.

Any school system which inaugurates such a program will be rewarded with ideas on how to improve public relations practices, reduce costs, save time, conserve materials, improve teaching methods, and insure more efficient operation of the school. Staff participation will increase, employee relations will improve, and individuals with creative imagination will be singled out and given the incentive to help make the system grow. Most important of all, a co-operative, united staff will help to insure the good will of the public.

13. *School Boards in Action*

THE SCHOOL BOARD occupies a unique position in the public relations program. Because of the nature of its organization and its limited interpretative role, the board is seldom publicized. Yet it is responsible for the education system in its entirety; therefore, its power and influence are tremendous.

It is the duty of board members to employ a superintendent and then to help him in every way in administering his many tasks. The superintendent must be given all powers which belong to him as chief executive. Members of the board must determine the policies to be followed regarding finance, the type of education to be provided; the salary scale for teachers, transportation plans, and other vital problems.

Long experience has demonstrated that the board should always act as a committee of the whole. A special committee may be appointed to investigate a particular problem, but it should be discharged when it has fulfilled its responsibility.

School board members should be fully informed on the following matters:

1. the taxing power of the board;

2. prevailing relations between the schools and the community;

3. trends in school population;

4. the assessed and true valuation of the district;

5. the per capita cost of education within the district;

6. statutory provisions regarding organization of the board, number of members, terms, and duties;

7. the value of opening all meetings of the board to the public;

8. the age and condition of school buildings, plans for new buildings, valuation of school property;

9. the educational philosophy of the school;

10. policies regarding retirement of teachers and other employees, use of school property for outside activities, purchase of equipment and supplies, insurance, and so on;

11. the necessity for becoming active members of an association of school boards;

12. the desirability of referring individual personnel problems to the superintendent;

13. the vital necessity that the board retain financial control of the school system.

Each member of the board should be an active public relations agent. If the board operates in an effective manner, each member will be thoroughly informed regarding the aims, problems, achievements, and needs of the schools. It is very important that each member be capable of translating his information to the people. This process is continuous in all of the varied contacts which the individual makes.

A school board member will be invited to many community gatherings. Often he is asked to speak or give his views on some school-community problem or proposal. This is an excellent opportunity for him to speak informally and yet officially to the public whom he represents on the board, and to present certain essential facts regarding the program of the schools.

The board member should become a human "listening post." In his varied contacts—whether in civic activities, lodge meetings, or parties at the country club—he will hear diverse opinions regarding the schools and their personnel. By being thoroughly informed, he can stop gossip and counteract misconceptions. Furthermore, he can inform the superintendent and other board members of possible conflicts and lack of understanding in certain areas, and together the superintendent and board may correct difficulties before a crisis occurs.

For the good of all concerned, it is essential that the superintendent and school board members work in harmony. They must remember that the welfare of the pupils, which is the true purpose of education, is above any personal interest. The following *School Board Members Creed* was suggested in the 1946 yearbook of the American Association of School Administrators:

"I will hold the superintendent of schools responsible for the administration of the schools.

"I will give the superintendent of schools authority commensurate with his responsibility.

"I will expect the schools to be administered by the best-trained technical and professional people it is possible to procure.

"I will elect employees only on the recommendation of the superintendent.

"I will participate in board legislation only after considering the recommendation of the superintendent and only after he has furnished complete information supporting his recommendation.

"I will expect the superintendent of schools to keep the board of education adequately informed at all times through both oral and written reports.

"I will expect to spend more time in board meetings on educational programs and procedures than on business detail.

"I will give the superintendent of schools friendly counsel and advice.

"I will refer all complaints to the proper administrative officer or insist that they be presented in writing to the board as a whole.

"I will present any personal criticism of employees to the superintendent.

"I will provide adequate safeguards around the superintendent and other personnel so they may perform their proper functions on a professional basis."

What about secret meetings of the board? There should be none, declares W. T. White of Dallas. "The public is very suspicious of secret proceedings," he says. "Although there are times when it is necessary for the superintendent of schools to have private conferences with the board, no official action should be taken under such conditions, and such conferences should not be held at a regular time.

"Stated meetings with the board and called sessions should be open to the public, to the newspapers, to school personnel, and to all others who may be interested. Any time the board and the administration close the door to the meeting room, the people who are on the outside become suspicious. They begin to think that the school board and the administration are hatching up some nefarious scheme which will not bear the light of day. As a matter of fact, such a condition rarely ever exists; but the school administration and the board of education must keep themselves free of suspicion by operating on an above-the-board policy."

School board members have a dual responsibility in the interpretative program. They must interpret community needs, interests, attitudes, and problems to the superintendent, principals, and teachers. At the same time, they must interpret the philosophies and activities of the system to the community.

Since board membership changes frequently, a training program should be set up for all new members. This orientation should emphasize the means by which they can make the most of their roles as public relations agents. Both the superintendent and the experienced members of the board must share in this responsibility. Occasionally, members are elected because of their strong beliefs regarding school policies or personnel. In situations such as this, new members should be careful to distinguish between conflict in policies and conflict in personalities. To be sure, there will always be differences of opinion on any board. That is altogether natural and democratic. But these differences need not result in suspicion and enmity. Conflict will not arise if members consider their differences objectively. Instead, understanding, appreciation, and tolerance of individual attitudes will result.

Members of a school board play a powerful role in the system's over-all public relations program. As the appraisal agency for the district, the board must study the educational needs and try to provide facilities to satisfy them. In addition, members must furnish information about the system to the public. As servants of the people, they will face problems and adversities, but their duties will bring them rich satisfactions and rewards.

14. *Students Make the Grade*

STUDENTS can be the most active agents in the public relations program, yet often they are the most neglected. Administrators and teachers take them for granted, and do not capitalize on the fact that students are eager to act as agents of good will for their schools.

Here are some of the ways in which students may become active public relations workers:

1. Through participation in assemblies, sports, music groups, forensics, publications, class organizations, and other activities.

2. By studying subjects and projects which show the relationships between the school and the community.

3. By participating in school-community programs with their parents.

4. Through their appearance on programs of civic, cultural, religious, and professional organizations of the community.

5. Through field trips, excursions, and other school-sponsored visits to places of interest in the community and in the region.

6. Through editorials, news stories, feature stories, cartoons, and photographs in the student newspaper and yearbook.

7. By sponsoring special assemblies with members of a particular civic club or group invited as honor guests.

8. By acting as guides and members of the greeting committee not only on special occasions but in day-to-day contacts as well.

9. By designing posters, and building exhibits and displays for use in stores and offices during the observance of American Education Week.

10. By linking school subjects with local businesses (for example, a high school journalism class may be invited to help in the production of the local daily or weekly newspaper).

11. By inviting a local group to a class or laboratory activity (a class in home economics might give a tea for mothers).

Few teachers realize the tremendous role daily classroom activities play in the public relations program. Nothing can be quite so harmful to public approval as tense student-teacher relations. Each student carries away a definite and lasting impression of the teacher. Learning can take place only in an environment of confidence, friendliness, and understanding. Evidence is accumulating that administrators and teachers are becoming more alert and co-operative in all relationships which elevate the understanding, trust, and appreciation of the school in the minds of the students.

Teacher-pupil relationships form the basis for attitudes of children. Does Miss Owen take a genuine interest in every child? Does she find time to help and counsel each one individually? Does she know something of the student's home life, his hopes and interests? Answers to these questions may determine whether or not the children understand and appreciate their school.

Ten years ago John Blank was graduated from Middletown High School. Today he is president of one of the leading civic clubs, takes an active part in church work, and works with Boy Scouts. He is one of the community "work horses." What is his feeling toward the public schools of his city? Whatever it may be, it began in grade school, where he received basic impressions and developed lasting attitudes. When viewed in this light, it is easy to see that special attention to today's pupils means better understanding and support from tomorrow's public.

Conduct of pupils, both in and away from school, influences the total public relations picture. That is why it is important that students be reminded of their responsibility as representatives of the school in whatever they do. This idea can be emphasized in the home room, by the student council, the school newspaper, and through other channels.

Parents should be fully informed about activities or programs in which their children take part. In arranging for a visit to an airport, for example, parents want to know why the trip is to be made, the method of transportation to be used, provisions made for the safety of the children, and other details. In many instances, the teacher can invite parents to help plan the trip and even accompany the students.

Children will like what they can understand. If they have a share in planning and taking part in school activities, they will like their school better as a result. More important, if they understand their school policies and like them, they become enthusiastic and active agents in the public relations program.

"Children's ideas are so ridiculous and impractical," a principal once said. To be sure, many of them are, but some good ideas will come out of any group. Better still, if time permits, it is well to allow pupils to try out their ideas to see for themselves if they will work. In a poll conducted recently by the Department of Elementary Principals of the National Education Association, 84 per cent of the principals who replied said that they used some form of student participation.

"The most popular people in any community are its children," someone once remarked. Their activities and programs are of deep interest to their parents and other citizens. For this reason, it is vital that they understand and enjoy their school experiences. Then they will report favorably to any person who asks them about their school.

In some communities, students have a voice in determining school policies. When students formulated the safety rules at a school in Missouri fewer pupils disobeyed them. In some schools, suggestions of all kinds are channeled through the student council, after which the sponsor and principal evaluate them. The children will conform to changes more co-operatively if they have had a voice in making them.

The principal and teachers should do everything possible in helping students to appreciate their school. By giving them a voice in programs, plans, and policies, they will become ambassadors of good will.

15. *Winning Alumni Support*

ALUMNI are probably the most ignored of all school publics. Too often students have been graduated and then practically forgotten by administrators and teachers. The support of future alumni must be won during their school years. Every school in a sense, of course, inculcates its students with the traditions, ideals, and purposes of the institution. The great need is for some integrated program by which loyalty and pride may be cultivated in the critical student days.

Administrators frequently forget that within a few years after graduation the alumni are voters with the authority to pass upon school requests. When they understand the programs, problems, and objectives of the schools, they become an interested group whose support can be enlisted.

How may alumni become a potent force in school progress? First, there must be a system of communication between the

57

graduate and his school. Former students should be kept informed through (1) news stories, (2) speeches, (3) exhibits, (4) letters, (5) motion pictures, (6) radio, (7) special bulletins, and other such media. Outgoing channels are more easily maintained than incoming ones.

The school should recognize its alumni as often as possible. Events such as dances, banquets, picnics, receptions, special assemblies, and class reunions should be held to honor graduates and former students.

Alumni should be urged to participate in many school activities. A representative group might aid in making curricular revisions. School facilities should be available at all times for use by groups of former students. They should be encouraged to establish special awards in such fields as scholarship, sports, music, and forensic activities. In many instances, parents of graduates and students have presented paintings, organs, libraries, and other gifts as memorials or class offerings.

The school system should offer extended services to its graduates. A vocational-guidance office might be set up, and evening classes could be held, emphasizing both regular subjects and topics of special interest.

It is far more effective to gain the support and loyalty of the student during his school days than to wait until school is no longer a part of his daily life. Mere casual contacts with students are not enough. Teachers must emphasize, through positive and clearly defined principles, the worth of the school system to all students. Each system should start a definite information program directed toward the student level. After all, much of the information which the general public has about the schools reaches the parents through their children. Students should know how their schools are supported, how they are organized, and the many services they render. Students in the higher grades should understand school finance, or at least the rudiments of it.

Naturally, a child who enjoys school and has reasonable success in his classwork and other activities will be favorably inclined toward the school—indeed, toward the entire system. But if he gets mixed up in his relationships with teachers, if he fails to understand what he is asked to do, if the whole experience is unpleasant, then he becomes a public relations agent who carries an unwholesome influence. Worst of all, he may be graduated or leave school carrying those attitudes with him. As an alumnus, his influence weakens the confidence and support of those with whom he comes in contact.

The student's loyalty toward his school is developed in a variety of ways. It may come from sports, school or social clubs, or individuals. Perhaps the deepest loyalties are those engendered by teachers whose influence carries far beyond the classroom. More teachers must see the alumni picture. If faculty members overlook the advantage of months or years of close association with students, it is almost impossible for the president of the alumni association to hope for much enthusiasm from graduates after commencement. Today teachers and staff members are coming to the realization that all their contacts with students—not just as club sponsors or as instructors in certain subjects—contribute to the alumni possibilities of tomorrow.

How are alumni received when they return to your building? Are they allowed to stray around on their own or are they greeted cordially and made to feel that they are welcome? Teachers, office workers, students, and nonteaching personnel should be on the alert for former students who return to the building for a visit. The atmosphere of every school should be that of genuine friendliness at all times.

One wise principal sends personal letters from time to time to graduates who he believes would be interested in special programs at the school. Quite a number attend the programs. "The main advantage," he says, "is that even though many cannot attend, they always appreciate our thinking of them."

Members of the high school alumni association should plan a variety of year-round activities. Yet social affairs alone accomplish little other than renewal of friendships. Evidence is accumulating that school administrators are realizing the worth of strong and active alumni groups and are discovering new ways of keeping interest and support at a high level.

59

16. *The Citizens Take Part*

UNDERSTANDING AND SUPPORT of the public schools will come only after interest in their welfare has been stimulated in the citizens of the community. This interest begins when the public is made a partner both in the planning and in the administration of the educational program.

Yesterday's school was community-centered. It had to be, of course. The teacher's salary was known by everyone, and the teacher in turn knew the problems and secrets of the families with whom he boarded. Social affairs were held in the schoolhouse. So were sports events when they were added to the list of activities. The school was the center for programs, political meetings, pie-suppers—in fact, about everything except religious services.

Then school systems began to expand. Superintendents and their board members planned larger facilities. New subjects were added to the course of study. Sports and extracurricular activities received a tremendous amount of attention. As a result, school costs skyrocketed.

What was Mr. Average Citizen thinking? Usually his own affairs kept him so occupied that he knew little about the many changes in the educational pattern. Sadly enough, school leaders did not keep their public informed. They took the support and understanding of the people for granted. Suddenly, as one superintendent expressed it, "I awoke to the realization that the public had no idea about the aims, problems, philosophies, and services of my system." The gulf between public and schools was a wide one.

Co-operation between public and schools is the guiding philosophy today. Evidence is accumulating that educational leaders are back on the right track. They are emphasizing understanding and participation as they broaden their public relations activities.

It is not enough that the people speak and that their voice be heard. That is the belief of Abel Hanson of Teachers College, Columbia University. Writing in the *School Executive,* he stated, "It is even more important that the quality of that voice improve, that deeper understanding of school problems be matured among all of the people. Better schools exist in communities where public esteem and understanding of what the schools are trying to do have reached high levels.

"This is no accident. Rather, it is because the superintendent of schools and his staff of teachers, encouraged by the board of education, have taken the real problems of the schools directly to the people for analysis and study. Lay participation of this kind is the most important single development in school administration in the last decade. It is also the most promising portent of better schools and deeper public understanding of education in the future."

Public confidence in schools will come as carefully planned programs of community-school co-operation are set in motion. In many systems, advisory committees of citizens have a part in developing the educational policy of the schools. Obviously, this practice does not reduce the responsibility of school board members and administrative officials. They must still make the final decision on all matters of policy. At the same time, committee members feel free to discuss and evaluate existing policies and make recommendations for improvements. Every suggestion is then considered and evaluated by administrative officials. Back of this procedure is the basic operating philosophy that the public must become a partner in school life and must also accept a greater degree of responsibility.

Few agents in public relations carry the dynamic force of an effective advisory committee. It is important that a citizens' group of this nature reflect the opinions of a full cross section of the community. Findings of several conferences and workshops show that it is necessary for such committees to include members of all religious faiths, both political parties, and parents, as well as citizens who do not have children in the public schools. Most of the effective groups also seek members with a variety of business and professional backgrounds.

61

Members should be elected from the major civic groups. In one city, representatives are chosen from the following organizations: the Ministerial Alliance, the American Legion, the American Legion Auxiliary, the Business and Professional Women's Club, the Lions Club, the Rotary Club, the Kiwanis Club, the Federated Study Club, the YMCA-YWCA, the city council, the Parent-Teacher Association, and various fraternal groups (a system is followed by which one representative is rotated among lodges of the city).

Each superintendent must know his community well enough to decide what groups should be represented on the committee. He will discover that most groups will co-operate enthusiastically. In fact, many of them long for a closer association with the school system.

What should be the first objective of a newly organized committee? It is obvious that committee members with varied backgrounds may have little in common at first. For that reason, it is well to begin with a fact-finding program. Committee members should devote several meetings to discussion and examination of known problems and situations. Then the group can decide upon an objective, preferably a tangible one. As as example, after studying the statistics and the needs, the group might recommend higher salary schedules. On the other hand, it is doubtful that the committee could make a worthwhile recommendation on such a complicated matter as a change in curriculum. Later, as the group gains in experience, it might well make valuable suggestions concerning such problems.

How often shall meetings be held? Most advisory groups meet once a month. Times for meetings vary: more than one superintendent is convinced that a luncheon meeting is the most successful. Members of civic groups are occupied with many affairs, so it is necessary to arrange a time convenient for them. Often they will attend a luncheon or dinner meeting when they may miss a morning, afternoon, or night session.

What subjects should be discussed at these get-togethers? The range is as wide as the school program and its public. Such topics as extracurricular activities, adult education, school regulations, teaching methods, and special staff programs might be considered.

A common denominator of all successful groups is "the ability, regardless of their organizational machinery, to co-ordinate the energies of other organizations in the community." That is the opinion of Henry Toy, Jr., director of the National Citizens Commission for the Public Schools, New York City. He adds, "Often committees whose members act simply as individuals are as successful in this as committees whose members each formally represent another organization.

"Simply by sending speakers to luncheon clubs, trade unions, and businessmen's associations, many citizens committees have won a tremendous amount of support for the schools. One citizen group we know of found that a great many civic, fraternal, and professional organizations in the community long had 'education committees.' By persuading all these groups to adopt similar objectives, the citizens committee won a great deal of support for the schools, a support that had always existed but that had been dispersed to the point of invisibility."

The work of hundreds of groups of citizens who are interested in improving the public schools has received a tremendous impetus from the National Citizens Commission for the Public Schools.[1] Formed in May, 1949, the commission acts as a clearing house to enable existing groups to benefit from the experience of others in the hope "that community efforts now being carried out in isolation can benefit from the continuing encouragement and pooling of information which the commission provides."

As one of its major activities, the commission co-operates with the Advertising Council, Inc., in a campaign designed to dramatize the problems and opportunities of public school education in newspapers, in magazines, on outdoor posters, and on radio and television. In brief, the commission has set for itself two immediate goals: to help Americans realize how important our

[1] The national headquarters of the commission are located at 2 West 45th Street, New York 19, New York.

63

public schools are to our expanding democracy, and to arouse in each community the will to improve its public schools.

State citizens committees are increasing in number. One of the most successful is the Ohio Citizens Commission for Public Schools, formally incorporated on December 6, 1949. The group, which has 29 members, is entirely dependent upon contributions of state organizations and business concerns. In addition to commission members, the Ohio organization has about 1,-600 "associates" who receive its publications. During its first year, the group established contact with approximately 50 community citizens committees. These are continuing organizations. Yet, important as are the national and state groups in promoting the work of schools, only community groups can make the necessarily detailed examination of local conditions in order to determine objectives and courses of action.

The advisory committee should never be considered a separate unit in the public relations program. It should play an important role in all activities—newspaper publicity, newsletters, P.T.A. programs, openhouses, and so on. In other words, it should be encouraged to identify itself with the school system, with its problems, needs, and progress.

Understanding comes with participation. The more leaders who take part in school-community relationships, the greater the understanding on the part of all citizens of the community. When lay advisers join administrators in evaluating, improving, and extending education, the moral and financial support of the community will increase.

The advisory board should make a continuing inventory of the needs of schools. In this way members of the group can spearhead every movement and develop new programs and facilities on the basis of their findings. Remember this: The best educational public relations program is one which is a co-operative project with both school personnel and civic leaders participating. As the schools grow in importance, so does the work of citizen committees.

17. *When Parents Become Partners*

WELL-INFORMED, ENTHUSIASTIC PARENTS can be effective agents in the public relations program. Parents play a vital role because they spread information and opinions regarding personnel, curricula, facilities, and other phases of school life throughout the community.

Most parents are eager to participate in school affairs when they know how they can help. For example, one of the newest practices of the schools is the maintenance of a "parents' talent file." A list is made of all parents who have abilities that may be utilized by the school and who are willing to take part. In addition, records are kept of assistance given to the school by the fathers and mothers on the list.

Administrators and teachers have discovered that a parent group may be helpful in establishing a new policy. In many communities, the advice and suggestions of the group are sought before the new policy is announced or set in operation. Certainly whatever the policy being considered—whether to change the grading system or to reduce the length of the school day—it must have the understanding and consent of the public before it can become effective.

A word of warning: Mr. J, the principal, should never seek the advice of parents in policy-making unless he means to consider their suggestions. He must be willing to present both sides of the issue, and, most important of all, he must listen sympathetically to the views of parents who disagree with him. Knowing that there will be differences in opinion on most issues, the principal must have enough leadership ability to guide staff and parents toward attainable goals.

No matter how large or small the school, the principal will depend upon certain key parents. They are the ones who must be informed regularly of new procedures and policies, and they in turn must keep the principal informed of changes in public thought toward the schools.

Of all community organizations, the Parent-Teacher Association is the most valuable ally of the school administration. P.T.A. is a going concern. It now has 5,000,000 members in 31,000 locals, and it is adding new units at the rate of 2,000 a year. It has become an important part of our school tradition. Its main purpose, of course, is to work with educators for the common good of the child. The fact cannot be overlooked that it is a powerful influence in community life because it has avenues of contact not available to other organizations. It reaches directly into the homes of those most interested in the welfare of the schools.

What are the objectives of P.T.A.? National headquarters state that its aims are "to promote the welfare of children and youth in home, school, church, and community; to raise the standards of home life; to secure adequate laws for the care and protection of children and youth; to bring into closer relation the home and the school, that parents and teachers may cooperate intelligently in the training of the child; and to develop between educators and the general public such united efforts as will secure for every child the highest advantages in physical, mental, social and spiritual education."

Typical projects and activities of the P.T.A. include study groups (in child psychology, school work and methods, and other fields)

> programs of parent education
> community projects
> school projects
> demonstrations of school activities
> social affairs
> entertainments
> presentations of gifts to the schools
> motion pictures
> founders' day celebrations
> musical programs

Like any other group, the P.T.A. unit will rise or fall on the merit of its program. Ideally, the program will meet some pressing local need. One group may sponsor a children's free dental clinic. Another may provide a summer park program. Locals in Flint, Michigan, operate a clearinghouse for children's outgrown clothing. In Cheyenne, Wyoming, several groups have collaborated to set up a model nursery school. These are examples of the many and varied projects carried out by parent-teacher groups all over the nation.

There are many professional and personal advantages to be gained through active P.T.A. membership. Among them are the following:

I. Professional advantages

  1. For the teacher and the school administrator

    A. An opportunity to take part in a nationally known and respected community organization.

    B. A better understanding of the needs of children and youth, derived from an acquaintance with their parents and from a knowledge of their home environment.

    C. A feeling of partnership with parents in the common task of guiding children toward sound development in mind, body, and character.

    D. A well-defined channel through which to exert a constructive influence in the community.

    E. An opportunity to learn about the community and its problems, particularly those affecting child welfare.

    F. A technique for explaining educational aims and methods to groups of parents.

    G. An understanding of the problems of home life and parenthood.

    H. Recognition of the importance of child welfare as a goal common to persons of all races, nationalities, religions, political interests, and economic circumstances.

    I. An opportunity to interpret problems of school administration to parents in order to insure their understanding and co-operation.

    J. The privilege of working with an organization that constantly seeks support, both financial and moral, for the schools.

    K. A chance to secure funds to finance new or additi[onal] educational services not provided by the local sc[hool] board.

    L. The opportunity to work with co-operative and [con]structive critics of school policy.

    M. A means to bring community needs and interests t[o] attention of all school personnel.

2. For the parent

    A. An opportunity to take part in a nationally known [and] respected community organization.

    B. A chance to become a better parent, and to become [more] understanding of all children.

    C. An opportunity to learn from teachers educati[onal] methods which will be effective in home training.

    D. A voice in determining the kind of education his [chil]dren shall have.

    E. Access to outstanding publications and expert opi[nion] on child welfare and on education for home and fa[mily] living.

II. Personal advantages

1. For the teacher and the school administrator

    A. An opportunity to meet the people of the commu[nity] on a friendly social basis.

    B. A chance to share in the joys and the struggles of [com]munity life.

    C. A sense of partnership and common cause with pa[rents] who are working for the welfare of their children.

    D. An opportunity to establish himself in the eyes of pa[rents] as an important contributor to community welfare.

    E. An opportunity to broaden his horizons far beyon[d] limits of classroom and school.

For the parent

A. An opportunity to meet the teachers on a friendly social basis.
B. An occasion to confer with teachers in the regular course of events, without embarrassment to anyone concerned.
C. An opportunity to watch the school at work.
D. An opportunity to become articulate regarding the educational needs of children and to express his convictions through group action.
E. An opportunity to broaden his horizons far beyond the limits of the home.

om the public relations point of view, these three powerful ps—parents, teachers, and administrators—can combine ert a tremendous influence in community life.

18. *Co-operation Is the Keynote*

THE MEANS by which a school system relates its ideals bjectives to other community groups are many and varied. are in daily use, while others are utilized periodically. though there may be a multiplicity of organizations in a nunity, school leaders recognize that they must synchronize programs as closely as possible with other agencies.

rtunately, the superintendent is in an excellent position ak community services to children's needs. He can keep aff informed about available services, bring the needs of ren to the attention of community agencies, and assist in dinating the services of all groups.

u may ask, "Don't we already have too many organizations e community without starting a community council? Why tilize existing groups?" The procedure to be set up will nd on the local situation. In general, the superintendent vork through existing channels. Even then he may realize eed for some type of co-ordinating council. For one thing, a council will prevent duplication of services and activi-

69

ties. Furthermore, it provides a clearance bureau for major educational projects. Most important, the influence of the group can be a powerful factor in molding favorable public opinion toward the schools and their needs.

If the community lacks such a council, the superintendent has an excellent opportunity to take the initiative in its organization. How should he proceed? Here are some questions which he must answer in the planning stage:

1. Which agencies and organizations can be counted on to contribute to the educational program?

2. What can be done by schools and agencies in improving the quality of daily living in the community?

3. How should members of the council be chosen? What community agencies should be represented on the council?

4. What services are now available in the community and who has charge of the various programs?

5. What part will the schools play and what part will community groups play in reaching the desired objectives?

6. What are some methods of informing community agencies and organizations of the needs of children?

7. To what extent can teachers be expected to help in the school-community program?

8. How many administrators and teachers are active members of welfare groups?

9. What overlooked areas of child-help need assistance from organized sources?

10. How can teachers discover child needs and report them to the proper agencies?

Alert school leaders no longer confine their public relations activities to interpreting education. Today they are devoting much time to building smoother working relationships with organized social agencies. Educators realize that each child is influenced by his total environment. His experiences in his Sunday-school class, on a scout camping trip, at the movies, at the municipal swimming pool—all these and more are sources of knowledge. These agencies must understand the school program and its objectives, and the school in turn must make the most of services provided by these groups.

Teachers, above all groups except the parents, know the needs of children. Theirs is the responsibility of reporting those needs to the proper agency. "But," someone may ask, "aren't all the needs—recreational, social, physical, financial, and others—being met by interested groups?" Look at the local situation. Freckled Jimmie, who sits on the second row, needs glasses. Mary is slightly deaf. And you've probably suspected that Fred isn't getting all the food he needs. To be sure, there may be agencies to care for these needs but teachers should call them to the attention of the operating groups.

Whatever the size of the community, whether it is a small village or a metropolitan center, school leaders must play active roles in co-ordinating services of the varied groups. With unity and understanding, school forces can unite with community agencies and provide real service for the children.

19. *Building Sound Community Relations*

THE BEST SCHOOLS are those in which the people of the community have confidence—confidence which comes from understanding and participation.

One superintendent was advised by a colleague from a nearby city that he should encourage his patrons to take part in the programs and activities of his school system. The superintendent replied, "Why, there is little telling what they would ask for. I'm afraid to risk it." Actually, no administrator can afford not to take the time to work with citizens and groups in the development of his program. It is imperative that school leaders remain alert to public attitudes and desires. At times, of course, the citizens may prefer certain practices which are educationally unsound. In such cases administrators must make it clear that there are certain problems of a professional nature which the public does not understand.

To be sure, there are risks in allowing and encouraging lay-men to work with administrators in developing school policies. On the other hand, in working with people of the community, the superintendent will find that as citizens gain a fuller under-standing of educational needs and services they will become eager to do more for the schools.

How can the superintendent make the most of all the groups and individuals who are working on a joint program? In what specific ways can he strengthen his community relations? How can a speakers' bureau be organized so that it will function ef-fectively? How can school facilities be used to bring the system and the community closer together?

Here is a check list which has helped many administrators to evaluate their efforts toward building better school-community relations:

1. Do you participate in community-wide programs?
2. Do you allow community groups (Boy Scouts, Red Cross, and others) to use school facilities?
3. Do you buy as many school supplies as possible from local firms?
4. Do you give priority to a local person when naming a new staff member?
5. Do you know key individuals of your community—the newspaper editor, the mayor, the president of the ministerial alliance, chairmen of civic groups, and others?
6. Do you telephone or write letters of appreciation to local civic workers who have performed outstanding services as citi-zens or leaders?
7. Do you encourage teachers and staff members to contribute to worthwhile community activities?
8. Do you ever present outstanding speakers or musicians as a special event for the entire community?
9. Do you join as many civic groups as possible?

SPEAKERS' BUREAU

Many school systems have organized speakers' bureaus in or-der to make teaching and administrative talent available to meetings of civic groups. Some suggestions for setting up the bureau follow.

1. Select members of the staff who are effective speakers and who are authorities on certain subjects.

2. Choose topics which will be of interest to the general public.

3. Establish a central clearance system for booking speakers.

4. Issue a pamphlet listing speakers, topics, and the time required for each speech. Send copies of the pamphlet to the president or chairman of each organization and institution in the community.

5. Hold a special meeting to brief the speakers on the program for the year. Emphasize the importance of the program and the contribution each speaker can make toward better understanding of the schools.

6. Provide a budget large enough to finance pamphlets, postage, and materials needed for talks and demonstrations.

7. Plan your offerings to include a large variety of programs. This will insure a balanced picture of the many phases of school life.

School Facilities

No longer are most school buildings closed three months each year, with every shade carefully drawn at the same angle as a sign of suspended operation. Rather, the modern school is following the plan of its forerunner, the village school, and is becoming a meeting place for the community.

1. Offer use of school facilities to all worthy organizations.

2. Develop a balanced program of work and recreation for groups using the buildings.

3. Plan a year-round program if possible.

4. Maintain a calendar of coming events in order to avoid conflicts.

5. Issue a community bulletin every week to inform patrons, teachers, and newspapers of programs to be held in the schools.

6. Establish clearly-defined regulations regarding use of buildings and facilities.

7. Make provisions for sufficient maintenance on the part of the custodians.

8. Allow groups using school facilities to share in the development of policies.

BUSINESS AND PROFESSIONAL ORGANIZATIONS

Local business and professional men can become active agents in your public relations program. What they think of you and your school system is most important. Too often they feel that they hear about school activities only when they can be of financial assistance. They are asked to run advertisements, in the school paper, contribute to the band uniform fund, or join in a co-operative advertisement just before an important football game.

What can be done to make them think favorably of the schools? Here are a few suggestions:

1. Pay all school bills promptly.

2. See that student salesmen for publications don't become "beggars of space" when they try to sell advertising.

3. Urge staff members to join the local chamber of commerce.

4. Explain tactfully when you cannot allow a local store to sponsor a commercial program in a school building during class hours.

5. Encourage teachers and staff members to become acquainted with the businessmen of the community.

6. Purchase supplies and equipment from local merchants whenever possible, and order articles made in another city through local businessmen.

7. Work closely with merchants who employ students on a part-time basis.

8. Exercise extreme care when using new furniture or other borrowed properties for school plays.

9. Deal tactfully with merchants whose business establishments adjoin school grounds, even though these "hangouts" are objectionable to administrators and teachers as well as parents.

10. Invite qualified business and professional men to take part in vocational guidance clinics.

11. Be ready for objections from certain merchants when vending machines are installed in school buildings.

12. See that students are co-operative and well behaved during excursions through local business plants. Do not expect merchants to hand out free samples of their merchandise to each group of students.

These are a few suggestions for building better understanding through community contacts. You have undoubtedly used many others which you have found effective. Be on the alert for new ideas, new activities, new ways of keeping your community school-minded. When you check results in public relations, you will find that the most potent and far-reaching element is an awakened public interest.

20. *Successful Financial Campaigns*

MANY SCHOOLS face a financial crisis today. The school dollar buys less, and with many elementary schools "bulging at the seams," more money is needed for buildings, teachers, and equipment. Citizens must be reminded of their obligations and responsibilities to their children and to their schools.

Where there is faith in education, there will always be financial support. This means that every request for school money must be justified. Superintendents and school board members must be aware of the many national, state and, local conditions which affect all phases of school support.

Wise use of school expenditures always results in better standards of living. Best proof of this is the report of the 1945 education committee of the United States Chamber of Commerce. In brief, this group found that states with the highest school expenditures also rank high in retail sales, life insurance in force, per capita income, circulation of national magazines, and so on. States ranking low in educational expenditures also rank low in these factors.

75

School leaders need not be apologetic in seeking adequate school funds. They can always marshal and present convincing evidence to show the need for increased financial support. Moreover, school administrators must demonstrate that wise management characterizes all financial and business affairs. This administrative practice is a must today. With the sharp competition for funds, the public is more critical of ways in which school money is spent. Student fees, once the main source of income, are being revived, usually with unfortunate consequences in public relations. Some fees may be necessary, of course, but the amount to be charged, the manner in which the policy is announced, and the expenditure of the funds are major considerations in seeking to gain public co-operation.

With the welfare of his public relations program in mind, the superintendent should compile and release financial information regularly. Too often the public is made aware of the needs only when an emergency occurs or when special projects are planned. Fiscal information should be accurate and complete, and it should be presented in an attractive and interesting fashion as well. Long columns of figures are dull and frightening. Yet school publications cannot be wholly pictorial. Between these two extremes lie methods of presentation which are dramatic, compelling, and factual.

Perhaps you are conducting a campaign for new buildings and equipment, or perhaps you wish to engage additional faculty personnel. But the buildings, facilities, and teachers are not ends in themselves. They have the ultimate purpose of developing the character and intelligence of the leaders of tomorrow. Thus the final objective of educational expenditure is to enrich human life.

A campaign is more than a drive for money. Over and beyond that goal is the educational value of the program. Citizens of your community will discover the needs, activities, and progress of your system. Therefore, the impact of the campaign is as important, and often more important, than its financial success.

Each fund-raising campaign is unique. To be sure, you may employ a speakers' bureau and other strategies used in scores of cities, but your local needs, your local situation, public opinion in your community—these and other factors make your project different from any other. For this reason, the planning of the campaign calls for creative and inventive thinking. Routine methods often fail because no study has been made of the specific requirements and problems of the situation. In order to be successful, a drive for funds must conform to the needs of the school system and the resources of the community.

You must sell *benefits,* not *costs.* You must create conviction on the part of the public. Without the faith of the people, all the public relations strategies in the world cannot guarantee financial support. When the public is convinced that the program is worthy, enlightened action will result.

Effective financial promotion cannot be accomplished by following a few A-B-C's of procedure. However, here are some suggestions which will help get results:

1. Determine the needs and the over-all objectives before the prospective budget is set up.

2. Make adequate provision for the cost of the campaign.

3. Plan a program to meet the needs, but be certain that it is attainable.

4. If the campaign includes a bond issue, see that all financial requirements are allowed for, in order that the public need not be asked to approve supplementary issues.

5. Be certain that school personnel fully understand the purposes of the campaign.

6. Select enthusiastic workers. They must be dependable, informed, personable, and tactful.

7. Enlist the co-operation of leading citizens and community organizations.

8. Pick an apt campaign slogan or theme.

9. Time the drive so that it will not conflict with others. Set up a time schedule for the campaign and see that it does not lag. The campaign will be more effective if compressed into a reasonably short time.

10. Get the project under way with a well-publicized rally,

and select a speaker for the meeting whose comments have influence in the community.

11. Use a uniform accounting system.

FUND-RAISING PUBLICITY

1. Assure the citizens at every step of the publicity program that the cause is worthy, that a real need exists, and that the community as a whole will benefit by the project.

2. Outline a list of possible feature stories, and save some of the best for the closing stages of the campaign. It is wise to gather stories from other communities showing what they have done or are doing with similar projects.

3. Use every publicity medium available in your community: press, radio, direct mail, billboards, automobile and window cards, posters, leaflets, personal interviews, speeches, exhibits, and so on. Be sure that all publicity has human interest value.

4. Seek the advice of newspaper editors, radio station managers, and other publicity experts in making your plans.

5. Avoid publicizing the campaign so far in advance that people forget its purpose and worth.

6. Publish results of the drive regularly.

7. Impress on all members of the campaign committee the need for their co-operation and enthusiasm. While publicity is a vital part of the drive, the ultimate success of the project will be determined by the efforts of the workers themselves.

GUIDES FOR A SUCCESSFUL BOND ISSUE CAMPAIGN

Twenty-five steps in planning and promoting a school-bond campaign have been outlined by Otis A. Crosby,[1] senior administrative assistant of the Detroit, Michigan public schools:

1. If possible, base the decision for a bond issue on millage increase on demands of the citizenry. Elect one of three premises, hope, fear, or shame.

2. Do a substantial research job tending to establish the rightness of the community's petition for a school campaign. Fix the

[1] *Campaigns Triumphant* (Chicago, The National School Service Institute, 1951), 3–4.

peak load in the elementary and in the high schools for a given year. Project the vacant property in terms of probable occupancy. Include any subtracting factors of school population such as parochial interests, and possible withdrawal of school-age children in years of lower income.

3. "Insist" on unanimous decision of the board of education establishing the call for an election.

4. Plan the campaign for a period in which schools are in session.

5. Early in the planning stages, administer a poll of opinion to all residents. It should cover the subjects of school services and an understanding of what schools are accomplishing. You may want to include such matters as class size, double sessions, qualifications of teachers, lunch services, auditorium facilities, community use of school buildings, adult education, driver training, and the like.

6. Create a Community Council for the Study of the Public Schools. Make it a committee of 100.

7. Based on their (favorable) findings, name an executive committee to "master mind" the campaign. Name subcommittees to cover every active phase of the campaign.

8. Take a long look at the election manners of your voting neighbors in surrounding communities. What has been the voting public's attitude towards supporting their public schools in your community? Break down the votes by precincts, and from that you may be able to determine the attitude of various groups such as labor, professional, business, and the like.

9. Establish a budget (not out of public funds) adequate to cover basic campaign expenses.

10. Early, take your employees into your confidence; ask their advice, and solicit their participation. Likewise, contact the press early by way of sounding them out.

11. Inventory organized opposition such as the real estate board, taxpayer groups, and, possibly, the chamber of commerce.

12. Counsel with the parochial interests at the outset of the campaign.

79

13. Withhold publicity except for an occasional story now and then. Do not reveal dates, and, if possible, withhold such pertinent information as the total amount of money sought until two or three weeks before the election when the campaign becomes a part and parcel of the public.

14. Thoroughly establish with all the workers the value of the important sales psychology, "What do I get out of it?" Pitch the appeal in every instance in terms of how the voting public is going to be benefited from better educational opportunities regardless of whether they have children in school or ever will have.

15. Insist that the campaign workers and the campaign literature observe the admonition, "Don't confuse the public with a mass of detailed facts."

16. In the main, pitch the appeal to women—85 per cent of the women make the vital decisions of the home.

17. Early in your planning, you must settle the argument, "Shall we tell the public how to vote, or merely furnish them unbiased information?"

18. While the campaign, as such, will be six to eight months or a year in the making, yet the campaign, in terms of public knowledge and participation, should definitely be limited to no more than three weeks.

19. Plan carefully the buildup of the three-weeks' campaign so that the peak comes 48 hours before election. After that, all activities should be shut off for 24 hours before election, and then a quick drive made for the last 24 hours before voting.

20. Committees which will carry a major part of the responsibility for the campaign will represent every facet of concern. Some of the more important committees will be those of: endorsements, telephone contacts, post-card barrage, transportation, finance, block organization, speakers, advertising, press releases, pupil activities, theaters and churches, parent associations, and parades.

21. At the outset of the active campaign, plan a poll of opinion to be staged about 14 days before election. Make the poll one of education, and, at the same time, one of fact finding.

Variations of the poll are to be found in a straw vote, and in the inquiring reporter.

22. The public press, and, in many instances, the radio will be relied upon heavily. Don't overlook the opportunities available through the letterbox, the question and answer column, the inquiring reporter, editorials, tie-in advertising, pictures, personal interviews, interesting and oftentimes humorous sidelights, and news stories prepared by alert newsconscious people trained for this job.

A number of short articles, each covering one point, are better than one long story for your newspaper.

Editors are invariably friendly toward copy that can be used by local firms in their advertising.

Professional and trade journals offer an excellent means of reaching business, labor, and other specialized groups.

Brevity in words, abundance of graphic materials, slogans, frequent repetition, eye-catching phrases, songs, and cartoons do much to spell out the message in little words with big letters.

23. Review moving pictures in the campaign field planned especially for school campaigns. A one or two-minute movie trailer may prove a good investment, although it is rather expensive.

24. About two weeks before election, plan to erect a large, neatly made sign on the site of each new building and where additions are contemplated. These signs might read something like this: "In an attempt to better serve the educational interests of boys and girls in this community, your Board of Education plans to build an elementary school, grades one to eight, on this site, work to begin as soon as funds are certified in the election of April 8."

25. The tone of the entire campaign should stress services to be rendered rather than costs to be assessed.

The campaign must be child-centered.
Emphasis must be placed on significant and obvious facts.
The language should be clear, simple, and nontechnical.
Pictures, charts, graphs, and slogans should be used.

It is poor economy to be stingy on the use of skilled professional advice, engravings, art work, and printing services.

Successful financial appeals require a special kind of psychology—a knowledge of what people are interested in, what makes them respond, what they consider worthwhile. School leaders must recognize the present sharp competition for public funds by more groups and agencies. They must create conviction in the minds of the public that the cause is worthy. They must be well informed and enthusiastic regarding their program.

Unfortunately, the subjects discussed in the preceding paragraphs do not cover the complete financial picture of the schools. School finance is always a mixture of many factors, influenced by state and local conditions. Each superintendent must carefully weigh every factor in his situation and then decide on a course of action. He must present a strong case if the schools are to keep pace with increasing demands.

When citizens approve a bond issue they deserve a word of recognition. Frequently they are forgotten in the many administrative steps which are necessary to get the new program under way. Some superintendents release a "thank you" news story to the press. Others send a personal note to those who were particularly active in the program.

Officials of the San Diego, California, city schools published an attractive pamphlet in the spring of 1949 entitled, "Thanks a Million for Your Millions." Filled with photographs, the pamphlet summarized the crowded conditions of the schools, explained the needs, told how San Diegans went to the polls in 1946 and voted a bond issue of $6,866,000, and then summarized the progress made on each item. The publication stated, "Here are the promises made in November, 1946. And here are the deliveries—paid for out of bond money, plus other budgetary funds." Such thoughtfulness is good insurance for the future.

21. *There's Magic in Print*

PRINTED MATERIAL can be one of the biggest guns in a school system's barrage upon the public. The purpose, the size of the community, and the cost are factors which must be taken into consideration in determining the type of material to be used. Unless ordered in large quantities, some kinds are not worth the cost.

Before making plans for printed matter, determine:

1. your objective.
2. the number of persons you hope to reach.
3. tentative copy angles and approaches.
4. the cost.
5. steps in planning.
6. the interests of the persons to be reached.
7. the manner in which the material is to be distributed.
8. the advantages and disadvantages of the method being considered.
9. the results of schools in which a similar method has been used.
10. the one person who will be given responsibility for the entire project.
11. the role the piece will play in the over-all public relations program.
12. some method of checking the effectiveness of the publication.
13. the time required to produce the material (the writing of the copy, printing, and distribution).

EFFECTIVE ILLUSTRATIONS INCREASE ATTENTION VALUE

The choice of illustrations for printed material is very important to the success of the publication as a whole. You must select illustrations which add to the total impact of your piece. Copy and art should be combined in a manner that will produce the greatest effect.

Pictures of an institution in use attract more attention than those of buildings alone. For this reason it is wise to show a stream of children entering or leaving a building. Avoid using a picture which contains so many figures, persons, or objects that the reader cannot grasp the situation immediately. Use this simple test: Glance at the picture briefly and then see if you can tell what is happening.

Readership studies of advertisements reveal that (1) the most effective pictures are rectangular, (2) on the average, a single big picture is the best attention-getter, (3) the silhouette is effective because it has no specific shape, (4) pictures at the top of the layout attract more attention than those placed at or near the bottom, (5) small pictures are more effective when they are placed close together in regular order (preferably numbered 1-2-3 or lettered a-b-c), (6) before-and-after pictures are exceptionally effective in attracting readers, provided the difference is graphic and easily distinguishable, and (7) line drawings, "arty" pictures, and drawings in woodcut usually get little attention.

Always choose illustrations which have easily recognized content and meaning and those which tie in with the copy and the theme.

Selling Ideas by Direct Mail

Selling by mail has a growing appeal for school leaders. Today Uncle Sam's postmen carry about eight and one-third billion pieces of advertising a year. What does this indicate to the school leader? Direct mail material issued by schools is in a highly competitive field. Thus it demands the best planning and presentation possible.

Here are six steps to success in direct mail:
1. Determine the objective.
2. Select carefully the names for the mailing list.
3. Determine the prospect's interests and desires.
4. Plan the copy so that it will meet the prospect's desires and at the same time include what you want him to believe.

5. Prepare copy and reply forms, if necessary.

6. Test the results.

Steps in Copy Preparation

1. Determine the action desired.

2. Choose a single dominant idea that will create the most interest.

3. Decide how your copy will tie in with the reader's interests from beginning to end.

4. Choose the format which is best for your purpose.

5. Make every word count toward reaching your objective.

6. Select illustrations which will attract interest and fit the theme of the copy.

7. Be sure that the copy is credible, frank, and friendly.

8. Test your first draft on a friend, relative, or colleague.

Use direct mail to:

1. stimulate and encourage staff members.

2. welcome new personnel.

3. win back inactive patrons.

4. develop interest in specified groups.

5. encourage attendance at school programs.

6. secure information from teachers.

7. solicit new ideas and suggestions.

8. build morale of staff members and parents.

9. keep in touch with parents.

10. correct present mailing lists.

11. announce new plans or policies.

12. capitalize on special events.

13. build better understanding.

14. increase income from all sources.

15. instruct staff members.

16. keep in touch with alumni.

17. prepare the way for home visitations.

18. acknowledge service and gifts.

19. explain special services to the community.

Yes, you are sending material to a list, but remember that it is individuals, not statistics, who will respond. What you write will be read by one person at a time. Use simple language. Prove your points. Use words to create pictures in the reader's mind, and be sure to make your copy specific: get down to cases, names, and incidents. The length of the copy should be sufficient to tell your story interestingly and forcefully. See that your printed material—no matter what its cost or aim—conforms to modern techniques of layout, illustration, and design.

Because of the great variety of printed media, the types which follow by no means exhaust the list. They are given to illustrate some of the principal channels which may be used in gaining public support.

I. Speech Reprints.

Often a speech given before a small group by an administrator or a teacher has ideas which should be carried to the general public or specific individuals. In this case, it is well to have copies of the address mimeographed or printed and sent to the readers you wish to interest. Costs will include (1) reproduction, (2) envelopes, (3) addressing, and (4) postage. It is well to consider the best method of distribution. A personal note from the superintendent attached to the reprint will increase its reader interest.

II. Post Cards.

Often called the "penny billboard" by direct-mail advertising experts, the post card has many attributes which make its use both valuable and flexible in school campaigns: (1) it presents a single reading surface upon which a message can be flashed to the recipient, (2) it requires no unfolding, and (3) it can be enlivened by illustrations which aid the copy and give it instantaneous appeal.

Results of surveys on the effectiveness of post cards show that those which use illustrations are approximately 30 per cent more successful than cards which rely on copy alone.

III. Reply Cards.

When seeking action in direct mail programs, use reply cards to speed up returns. If the card is enclosed with a letter, be sure to call attention to it.

1. Gear the card's copy to that of your letter.
2. Make every word earn its space.
3. Keep the tone tactful, friendly, and considerate.
4. Make it easy for the recipient to act.
5. Be specific in your instructions—"Mail the card today."

IV. Leaflets.

Step up the impact of your public relations letters by enclosing a leaflet in each. Tests show that the leaflet usually increases the response as much as 25 per cent. It gives more particulars and proof that can be put into a letter. Copy must be the best you can make it. Action photos will have great appeal, and a two-color piece will accentuate the proposal. Believe it or not, advertising experts have found that an attractive leaflet is usually retained longer than a letter.

V. Special Student Booklets.

Often the schools must get over certain ideas to students which are not included in the list of regular offerings. Teaching safety, for example, is a never-ending project at all levels of the public schools. You may use talks, films, exhibits, and other media, and you can certainly take advantage of effective printed materials as well. Two excellent examples are *Cycle Sense in Santa Fe* and *Dum Dum Teaches Safety,* both of which are issued under the direction of T. C. Bird, superintendent of the Santa Fe, New Mexico, city schools. Each has attractive illustrations, carries a powerful message, and is written in a language easily understood by children.

In planning this type of publication, always think in terms of the children, the potential readers. What would appeal to them? In what form would it be most attractive? What types of illustrations would be most suitable? Use plenty of illustrations and keep the copy brief and full of punch.

VI. Handbook for Teachers.

A handbook can do wonders to make the teacher feel at home

in the school system. Moreover, it can answer many questions which the new teacher may have in mind about the system and the city. A cordial welcome from the superintendent opens the handbook published by the Tulsa, Oklahoma, public schools. Topics discussed in this publication include reports to parents, a history of the system, teacher insurance, mail service, a directory of churches, adult education, bus routes, state aid, vacations, the school calendar, annual contracts, museums, and other information. Action pictures and sketches make the layouts attractive.

Generally speaking, this type of publication is best planned by thinking in terms of all questions which the beginning teacher would ask. Complete information and an attractive format, plus a friendly tone, combine to make this type of handbook exceptionally welcome.

vii. "Thank You" Booklets.

Often we inaugurate a big campaign to ask the public to support a certain program. But when the citizens approve the project do we say "thank you" in printed form? "Thanks a Million for Your Millions," mentioned above, is an example of an effective message of gratitude to the public.

viii. Calendars.

An attractive calendar can be of distinct value in the public relations program of a school system. Typical of this form of interpretation is the "Around the Clock Calendar" which was issued by the public schools of Rochester, Minnesota. Teaching days for the year are indicated, as well as all school holidays and special events such as dates for registration and commencement. The calendar, 19½ by 31 inches, has a background mosaic of 45 pictures depicting different phases of school life in Rochester, including sports events, library work, class work, and extracurricular activities. The focal point is a large clock, in the center of which is a picture of an attractive girl in cap and gown.

ix. Tickets.

Thousands of tickets are used for sports events, musical programs, plays, and other events in a typical school system each year. Why not use a special message on the backs of these? You can put across compact ideas to many citizens in this fashion.

x. Posters.

Posters are valuable in publicizing both special events and routine services. To make them effective, keep the following suggestions in mind:

1. Plan the layout to have space for at least one illustration, whether picture or drawing.

2. Strive for simplicity by limiting the number of ideas and elements.

3. If possible, use color to attract attention.

4. Leave plenty of white space.

5. See that the lettering is dignified, modern, and attractive.

6. Refrain from using trite, worn phrases.

7. Decide where the posters will be displayed before making your order.

xi. Transit Advertising Cards

Advertisers often allow use of their transit cards to community institutions, programs, and campaigns. Staff writers of an advertising agency may prepare the copy, but they will welcome ideas from school leaders. As in posters, the copy must be brief. Remember that a simple message is the most forceful technique for reaching the public. Because of the curvature of the card, you will find more headlines at the bottom than at the top. As always, select attractive illustrations which are related to the copy.

xii. Programs.

A great many programs, issued in a variety of forms, are distributed by every school system each year. In designing a program, first determine the readers. Then combine the best art and typography (and the best paper) possible. The main thing to remember is that each program creates a definite impression. Make it a positive one. See that the program carries its share of the public relations load.

Often the extra space on a program may be used to get over certain basic facts regarding the school system. One side of a program for the senior high school play, for example, will carry the title, members of the cast, name of the director, credit lines, the time, place, and other information. On the other side it might be wise to carry a headline "Did You Know?" followed by several interesting facts about the activities, achievements, and needs of the school system. This same idea may be used for football programs and similar types of printed matter.

xiii. Tabloid Folders:

Public relations experts know this fact: Material aimed at the general public must be written in a simple language, must use a minimum of facts, and must utilize cartoons and other telling devices. This material is a far cry from the slick, professional, expensive, and much too academic publications issued by some superintendents and principals. Rather, it is aimed at the masses of people, the great majority of whom prefer caricatures with very little accompanying text. Hit a few basic ideas hard with stirring illustrations and compact copy. Because this material is used in giant quantities, it can be printed on newsprint or a similar grade of paper. Carefully designed tabloid folders get results.

xiv. Pamphlets for Parents.

Close co-operation between the home and school is a necessary factor in the successful growth and development of children. With that thought in mind, quite a number of systems publish some type of pamphlet for parents of elementary school children. Typical of this type of public relations material is one issued by the San Diego, California, city schools. Contents include a foreword by Superintendent Will C. Crawford, a calendar of the school year, admission requirements, school boundaries, class organization, annual promotions, report cards, a time schedule, required attendance, absence procedure, textbooks and supplies, care of personal property, the school nurse, the cafeteria, traffic safety, school transportation passes, supervision of school playgrounds, school camping program, instrumental music, school savings program, library service, visits to schools, parent-teacher organizations, and summer vacation suggestions. Increased understanding and co-operation always come from the use of this type of publication.

xv. Subject Pamphlets.

"It was different when I went to school." That is a common reaction of many parents when they hear how their children are being taught certain subjects. To reduce misunderstanding and to get the co-operation of parents, scores of school systems now publish special pamphlets on their methods of teaching various subjects.

Readin', 'Ritin', and 'RITHMETIC! is the subject of a pamphlet issued by the Oakland, California, public schools. The copy points out that the program of the modern school differs in many ways from the schools which the parents attended, and that certain changes have been made because modern life demands a different kind of arithmetic. The entire pamphlet stresses the fact that the modern program of arithmetic has been streamlined and made more efficient. As a result, the child is taught things which he can put into use, facts which are related to the world in which he lives.

xvi. Staff Directory.

No matter what the size, every school system should issue a staff directory. It will be of value to employees of the system, and it will be helpful to parents and to the general public.

The Fort Wayne, Indiana, public schools issue, for example, a directory of the schools and public library. Contents include a calendar for the school year, holidays and vacations, the monthly report schedule, the tuition pay roll schedule, officers of the board of school trustees, administrative officials, non-academic personnel, supervisors, principals and faculty members (including the subject each one teaches, his home address and telephone) listed by schools, staff members of the bureau of research and measurement, instructors of the evening vocational classes, library staff members, and an alphabetical index of teachers.

xvii. Kindergarten Booklets.

The attitude of parents is of great importance to the ultimate happiness of children. This is especially true of parents whose children are entering kindergarten for the first time. The wise school administrator can accomplish a great deal by suggesting ways in which parents can assist school personnel in preparing these young citizens to become happily adjusted to their first school experiences.

Off to School, issued by the Des Moines, Iowa, public schools, achieves this purpose. Topics include the purpose of the book, the parents' responsibility in preparing their children for school, rules regarding eligibility for entrance, the daily program, safety suggestions, hints on health, desirable types of clothing, school experiences, the value of conferences between teachers and pupil, parent and child, and teacher and parents, the value of co-operation, and a check list for parents.

xviii. Press Relations Handbook.

What shall we tell the public? What kinds of pictures do newspapers want? Where do we find news? How are news stories written? These and other questions will be asked by the teacher who is assigned the task of reporting the news from her building.

An excellent way to answer these questions is to issue a handbook to school representatives. *How to Wiggle Your Nose for News,* issued by the Department of Planning and Information of the Dearborn, Michigan, public schools, is an example of how to train members of the teaching staff to become reporters. Topics include the value of school news in the over-all public relations program, Belmont Farley's list of the questions people have about their schools, picture possibilities, preparation of stories for the staff newsletter and national magazines, sources of news, the importance of deadlines, and the elements of news style.

xix. Speakers' Bureau Pamphlets.

Many systems operate speakers' bureaus, but few publicize the fact. John F. Locke, director of community relations of the

Cincinnati, Ohio, public schools, issues a special pamphlet on the purposes of their speakers' bureau. He emphasizes that the bureau is planned especially for civic and luncheon clubs, Parent-Teacher Associations, and other educational groups and church organizations. "Let us help plan your year's program— all service is free," the booklet emphasizes. Forty-three topics with names, titles, and telephone numbers of the speakers are listed.

22. *Letters Win Friends*

WELL-PLANNED LETTERS pay tremendous dividends in building good will and support. You must realize that every written word from you or your staff will contribute something to your reputation and to that of your system.

The effective letter has at least five basic objectives: (1) to get attention, (2) to arouse interest, (3) to create desire, (4) to establish conviction, and (5) to get action. These objectives can be reached even in a brief message. At first this task may seem impossible to you. But keep trying, and soon you will develop the knack of making every letter a good one.

First, determine the purpose of your letter. If you are hazy on this point, you are likely to jot down ill-chosen words, confused sentences, and long paragraphs. Without a purpose your efforts will be aimless. Have something to say. You are not writing letters to kill time or merely to be friendly. Say something that interests and intrigues the reader. Move over on his side of the fence before you start: discover what he is interested in, what he would like to do, why he will be interested in your letter. By knowing his way of life, his interests, and his problems you will have the key to the contents of the letter you are about to write.

Second, visualize the action you want taken. Think in terms of the response you desire. Do you want the recipient to attend a P.T.A. meeting? Are you asking him to contribute to the fund to purchase new uniforms for the band? Would you like for him to distribute special school promotion material to employees of his organization? No blanket appeal could possibly accomplish any two of these objectives.

Say everything you have to say, but make it brief! A lecturer on letter writing once asked an audience, "If words were dollars, how many of them would you waste?" Any reader resents a letter that requires him to wade through a mass of unnecessary verbiage simply because the writer was too lazy or careless to present his ideas concisely. "Word wasters" are common. Letter experts have estimated that the average letter carries at least 30 per cent excess weight in the form of unneeded words. You can write a long, rambling letter with little or no forethought. A compact, well-organized letter requires planning. Almost three centuries ago Blaise Pascal displayed an awareness of this truth when he apologized to a friend: "I am writing you a long letter because I have not the time to write a short one."

Use language the recipient will understand. It is not likely that he is acquainted with the jargon of education. Moreover, no matter what his station in life he will prefer short words to long ones. So don't say "contemplate" when you mean "plan" and don't say "superabundance" when you mean "excess." See that your sentences and phrases are clear.

No sentence in your letter is more important than the first one. Yet this is probably the weakest spot in the structure of the average message. If the opening sentence is interesting and significant, the recipient reads on. But if it gets off to a slow start, the attention of the reader will wander. In fact, he may read the first sentence and then toss the letter into the wastebasket. As Sherman Perry advises, "Put the reader in the letter right at the beginning." The opening sentence or paragraph is your initial contact. Always remember that the public to whom you write—whether it is enthusiastic or indifferent—is composed of human beings. Make your letters personal. Think of the readers as individuals, not as groups or statistics.

Avoid the participial opening. It is so easy to start with the words "referring," "answering," or "replying." The moment you do this you will find it difficult to end your thought at a logical point and you will use many extra, useless words.

"Should I try to be clever in my letters?" is a question that often comes my way. A certain amount of cleverness will strengthen the average letter, will make it unique and interesting. On the other hand, when you are searching for a different way to express yourself you may stray far from the point you are trying to make. Indeed, it is better to be trite than to be so clever that your thoughts are hidden.

Put your reader on a pedestal. A great many books and magazine articles have stressed the "you" attitude, the presentation of each message from the reader's point of view. Few school administrators follow this advice. Most of them still cling to the habit of telling their readers what the schools need, rather than emphasizing the benefits which will result for the reader. The reader will respond to an appeal which corresponds to his personal desires. So study him—find out what interests him. Then study your proposal and discover how it can tie in with that interest.

Be sure that each message is complete. In each instance, give your reader all the facts he will need in order to take the action you are trying to stimulate. You can easily defeat your purpose by omitting some necessary detail. Read the first draft of your letter and then ask yourself, "Have I answered all the questions in the mind of the reader?" Any situation that justifies writing a letter at all justifies writing a complete one.

Every piece of school correspondence has two potentialities. It can be either a builder of good will or a source of antagonism. Schools mail hundreds of letters which are certain to irritate the men and women who receive them. Often the offensive element is not the information itself but the manner in which that information is conveyed. Without realizing this, scores of school personnel use distasteful words and phrases or make negative implications which stir the resentment of the average reader. Therefore, knowing what to say is only half the job of the letter writer: knowing how to say it is the other half. Test your letters on yourself. Do they contain irritating expressions, tactless statements? Or do they show the reader all the courtesy and consideration that you would expect if you were in his place? Always consider the effect of your words on the reader and you will be more careful in your phraseology. Read over letters before you mail them to be sure that you have said what you intended, that no thoughts may be misinterpreted, and that nothing is offensive.

Many school letters lack pep and spirit. If you are tired, indifferent, or "in the dumps," those moods will be reflected in your letters. Flavor them with enthusiasm and they will have more reader interest.

The final factor of importance is the closing sentence. Always conclude your letter when its momentum is at the peak. Make the conclusion good—it will create the final impression.

Have you taken a good look at your outgoing mail recently? Are the letters as neat and attractive as they should be? You may find that their physical form detracts from their effectiveness. Remember that your letters are ambassadors of good will. They must represent your school favorably.

Letters, of course, can never substitute for the personal contacts of administrative officials and teachers. But wisely used, they can strengthen the public relations program.

Here are letters which an administrator can use to build good will:

1. Welcome: to new colleagues, staff members, or teachers
   to new citizens
   to newly appointed ministers

2. Acceptance: of invitations to meetings, banquets, lectures, sports events, and entertainments
   of invitations to serve on committees, councils, or boards
   of membership in professional, civic, fraternal, or religious organizations

	of resignations from positions, boards, committees, and planning groups
	of invitations to speak
3. Apology:	for absence from meetings
	for delay in acknowledging favors or courtesies
	for delay in sending promised material
	for inability to keep appointments
4. Appreciation:	to colleagues, principals, teachers, and secretaries
	to outstanding community workers
	for assistance in school programs
	for luncheons
	for messages of condolence or sympathy
	for messages of congratulation
	for personal favors or services
	for valuable suggestions
5. Acknowledgment:	of committee reports
	of complaints
	of scholarships, gifts, or memorials
6. Congratulations:	upon awards, accomplishments, or honors
	for outstanding service
	for promotion
	upon articles, speeches, projects, or books by staff members
7. Sympathy or condolence:	to professional associates
	upon the death of a teacher, former teacher, or former employee of the system
	to parents upon the death of a son or daughter
	upon injury or illness
8. Granting:	requests for business appointments, copies of addresses, booklets, or reports

information
use of school facilities

9. Declining:
    invitations to luncheons, banquets, lectures, or other gatherings
    invitations to serve on committees or boards, or to join organizations
    requests for information or material
    support of organizations or movements
    use of school facilities

10. Invitation:
    to colleagues, principals, or teachers
    to give addresses at meetings
    to attend special events
    to serve on committees

11. Recommendation:
    of associates or employees
    of former employees
    of personal friends
    of students or former students

12. Seasonal good wishes:
    to colleagues, staff, and teachers
    to parents
    to school board members

For example, did you ever write

a note of thanks to the editor for his generous use of school news?

a few words of appreciation to a bus driver for his safety record?

personal Christmas greetings to retired teachers of your community?

a letter of recognition to a church youth leader for his outstanding work?

letters of gratitude to P.T.A. presidents for their leadership?

All these and more are opportunities for thoughtfulness. By taking time to recognize these courtesies, any administrator can enrich both his professional and his personal life. Friendliness begets friendship. Write more effective letters and you will be amazed at the results.

23. *Broadcasts Bring Results*

MANY CHANGES are necessary to gear public school broadcasts to the rapid pace of modern competition. They must hold the listening audience, they must be planned and presented in the public interest, and they must be designed as professionally as possible.

Every radio listener has his choice of Bach or jazz, Haydn or hillbilly music, drama or quiz show, sermon or soap opera. So the school administrator must analyze the reception of each broadcast in terms of the competition it faces.

No one will deny that any worthwhile program must be planned with care. The director must know what he wants to accomplish during the allotted broadcasting time. When his idea is formulated, he must find the best workers available to carry it out. There is no reason why amateur talent cannot be used effectively, provided the rehearsals are given time and attention by a competent director.

Consider these factors in planning broadcasts:

I. The extent to which a school can utilize radio depends upon
   1. the size of the system,
   2. the objectives of the program,
   3. the cost of the production,
   4. the nature of the broadcasts,
   5. the trained leaders and talent available,
   6. the local radio situation.

II. Important characteristics of successful broadcasting are
   1. listener interest,
   2. intelligent showmanship,
   3. good writing,
   4. proper approach to the subject,
   5. proper casting.

III. Types of broadcasts are
   1. talks,

2. musical programs,
3. drama,
4. round-table broadcasts,
5. programs from classrooms,
6. interviews,
7. audience participation,
8. spot broadcasts of events,
9. quiz programs,
10. sustaining or "public service" programs presented by the radio station on free time in fulfillment of the requirements of the Federal Communications Commission.

Your program promotion will be strengthened by the use of a provocative title. Select one that attracts attention and has a close tie-in with the nature of the program, and one that will fit into the program lists in the newspaper. Perhaps one of your broadcasts is designed for adults. A title such as "Adult Education" is flat and uninteresting. Why not call it "Lifelong Learning" or something equally catchy.

Include people other than students and school personnel on your programs. If you select influential citizens who have effective radio voices to take part in your broadcasts, the program will have a variety of voices, it will have the aspects of community-wide interest, and the listener appeal will be stronger. Obviously, the speakers are allied with the interests and objectives of education.

Select one basic theme and concentrate on it. In many instances, the school public relations broadcast tries to cover too many topics. One central idea, projected in an interesting and professional manner, will result in a better program, and its retentive value will be much higher than a catch-all program.

Remember, too, that your appeal to listeners should be through the heart rather than through the head. You must arouse admiration or approval by the careful use of emotional overtones in situations, script, music, voices, and other media. Wise use of emotional forces will move the listener to take the action desired.

Your broadcast should have as wide an appeal as possible. Radio programs are heard by all types of people, among whom will be men and women who may not be especially interested in school activities. It is always best to plan a program on the assumption that the prospective listeners will have no interest whatever in the coming broadcast. What will interest them? What will catch their attention and hold it? Answer those two questions and your program is likely to influence those who hear it.

Learn all you can about the potential listening audience. Some of the wealthiest and most influential citizens, for example, probably send their children to private schools. And don't forget the many citizens who have no children attending the schools. Yet both of these groups are taxpayers—they have investments in the schools and their facilities.

Ordinarily, you do not present a broadcast just for the sake of having something on the air. You should have a definite objective when you take radio time. Never allow an effective broadcast to leave the air without a last-minute summary, a restatement of ideas, or an appeal to action. If your listeners do not act upon your presentation, then they are of no great value to you. Be specific. Tell the listener just what to do and how to do it, and make it easy for him to act at once. If you don't do this, he may lapse from his "almost ready" attitude into indifference.

What about talks? They can be overdone and they can be too long. A radio talk must have general interest and appeal, and it must be written and delivered in conversational style. Since the talk is meant for the general public, it should be written in simple language. "The best talk," a radio producer once said, "is written to inform and not to impress the listener."

Watch the timing of the script. If the talk is well constructed, it builds up to an effective conclusion. But if the timing is off and the speaker is cut off before he has finished, the whole object of the message is lost.

Never run two speeches together. If two talks are necessary, use musical numbers before, between, and after them. And even then, do not allow either talk to be too long. Remember that the listener wants entertainment and inspiration, not mere facts and figures. The best broadcasts are those which pull listeners, not those which are only "plugs" for the school system.

Take a tip from the networks and publicize your forthcoming broadcast. Make use of displays, school newspapers, bulletins, posters, city newspapers, announcements at meetings, photographs, letters, and other channels. Get advice on this matter from those who handle publicity at the radio station.

An effective school broadcast will influence the listener, as an individual, in his attitude toward the educational system. It should develop friendly understanding, show the importance of education, impress the listener with the type of program being emphasized in the system, and inform him of the benefits that education gives to individuals and society.

Program content should always be planned on the highest professional level. For this reason, the "disc jockey" type of program must be avoided. Choice of the type of production will depend, of course, on the audience you wish to reach and the availability of talent. Planned with the highest degree of technical skill, the school broadcast can have universal appeal.

24. *Television Time Is Here*

TELEVISION is on the march. The number of stations is increasing, and the amount of sets in use has shown a phenomenal rise. As the audience for this new method of communication grows, how can the schools take advantage of its potentialities?

Like radio, television eats up material at a tremendous rate. This means, of course, that producers will look to schools for promising ideas. This new medium is a unique and effective device for supplementing classroom instruction, providing in-service training for teachers, and giving the public a picture of what the schools are doing.

As in the case of radio, the person in charge of school television programs should seek to build friendly relations with the station personnel. In this way both the station and the school can share in the preparation and production of the programs.

In a recent article in *Techniques,* Allen H. Wetter, assistant to the superintendent of schools in charge of school-community relations, Philadelphia, Pennsylvania, stated the following important factors in dealing with television production:

1. The support and enthusiasm of the board of education, the superintendent, and his staff are necessary.

2. A television committee should be appointed which includes administrators, radio staff members, teachers, P.T.A. leaders, and others.

3. Over-all planning conferences must be held regularly.

4. There should be an immediate but modest beginning.

5. Effective programs require time, patience, and energy.

6. An effort should be made to see that all programs are desirable.

The television program should

1. give an accurate picture of the schools and enhance their integrity. Never before has there been so great a need for making known the achievements of the schools and for enlisting public enthusiasm, loyalty, and support.

2. encourage teachers and students to develop and improve classroom methods and projects.

3. offer supplementary learning materials and avocational ideas to students and adult observers.

4. provide entertainment. The stations face the hard facts of television life. A twist of the dial removes a dull picture.

School television programs should be publicized through notices sent to homes, student publications, P.T.A. newssheets, releases to the press, and announcements in the classroom.

Little can be written about ways in which schools are using television because only a few have worked with the medium, and those who have are still experimenting. Television, even when it reaches a maximum stage of efficiency, cannot match live drama and personal presentations, but it may become the next best thing. The new medium will give educational leaders an opportunity to show various phases of school life to great numbers of people, to demonstrate procedures in actual operation, and to offer an interpretative study by means of these demonstrations.

Here are some questions to be answered when a television program is being considered: (1) What is the purpose? (2) What form of presentation will be used? (3) What will be the major theme? (4) Who will write the script? (5) Who will be interested in the subject being considered? (6) Does the subject lend itself to several types of visual material? (7) Can the idea be presented in such a way that there is continuous action before the camera? (8) Is there ample time for a sufficient number of rehearsals? (9) Can the proposed production compete with the professional video entertainment offered by networks and local stations?

Producing an effective television show requires planning. Experts at the station will do most of the work in putting the show together. But you can do your share more effectively by understanding the problems of script preparation, music, lights, cameras, and so on. You must realize, for example, the physical limitations for some types of productions. Cameras and other facilities may be restricted. As a result you must economize on the number of sets and scenes for a program. In brief, the more you know about timing, acting, photographic methods, and all elements which make up this newest medium, the more workable ideas you will have to talk over with the producer.

The ideal television program must have entertainment value. This means that the public relations objectives must be woven smoothly into the pattern of the program. Obviously, you must maintain eye-and-ear interest at the same time you are seeking to project certain ideas.

As the television audience grows, all program producers will be forced to offer higher quality programs. As some observers have pointed out, originality will be encouraged as the field becomes more competitive. For most folks television still has the thrill of something novel and exciting. As a result, people watch their sets for long periods. But when the new wears off, the audience will become more selective both of the types of programs they watch and the amount of time they devote to the medium.

"Do not oversell," is the warning of television experts to advertising copywriters and others who prepare program material. This same advice should be remembered by those planning or directing an educational telecast.

No one knows exactly what effect television will have on public relations approaches used in publications, exhibits, radio, and other channels. It is still in the embryonic stages of development. Certainly it is here to stay, and you may be sure that it will have a profound effect on the public mind. Television programs must have the same quality of mass appeal as that of the best radio programs. Furthermore, school leaders must realize that their message can be toned down in narration in order to let the picture create the impact. School public relations personnel should give special attention to all types of television showings and thus find ideas which can be used in their programs. "Visual broadcasting" is unique—its real power and possibilities are yet to be revealed.

25. The "Eyes" Have It

WHEN YOU come right down to it, visual aids are about the best and quickest media for transmitting ideas and facts. In this restless age, people want to see something in a hurry. As a result, more and more school officials are using slides, film strips, motion pictures, and other aids in a variety of ways.

Like any other public relations tool, the visual aid must be chosen to meet a specific situation. It cannot usually carry the whole burden of the program. Yet it can strengthen the program as a whole. A motion picture, for instance, can be linked with direct mail, exhibits, brochures, news stories, speeches, and broadcasts in a special campaign.

Highest professional standards should be followed in using any visual aid. For example, slides which reveal that they were made by amateurs cannot carry the impact of those which are made to conform to the highest standards.

The suggestions which follow may serve as guideposts when certain types of aids are being considered.

I. Slides.

Slides can usually be shown successfully in most auditoriums without completely blacking out the room. They are adaptable to varying audience situations, for slides may be added, withdrawn, or rearranged as needed. They are inexpensive to make and are effective in color. Their storytelling possibilities are great. The following questions should be kept in mind as the project gets under way: (1) For what audience is the showing planned? (2) What is the purpose of the program? (3) Have all the scenes been outlined?

II. Film Strips.

Film strips are adaptable to pictures, charts, and drawings. The projector is small, light, and convenient to carry. The strips are adaptable to every type and size of audience. They can be mailed for a few cents and can be reproduced inexpensively. The film strip is also excellent for telling a story, and it is active in stimulating thought and discussion.

III. Opaque Projectors.

"A picture is worth a thousand words." This statement is truer today than ever before. The projected picture has the advantage of centering the complete attention of an audience on the subject presented. Opaque projectors are adaptable to innumerable subjects. The room must be dark. There are three available sizes to show material: 6x6 inches, $8\frac{1}{2}$x11 inches, and 11x11 inches.

IV. Films.

School movies have come of age. In the past few years they have taken on some of the style, arrangement, and effectiveness of both the industrial and the Hollywood productions. Good films put across ideas quickly. They can entertain, inform, instruct, and persuade. Best of all, retention of the material is high. A good motion picture is well worth the amount of time required for its planning and production. Quality should be your goal. Here are some factors to keep in mind:

1. To be effective, a film must be well done. It must compete with the best shown at theaters; it must have quality because it is promoting quality; and it must have professional planning and direction if it is to produce the desired results. Ideally it should have color and sound, and it should take no longer than thirty minutes and not less than twenty minutes to show.

2. Careful planning must always precede production. Facts must be gathered from many sources, objectives must be decided upon, types of audiences must be chosen, distribution plans should be discussed, and the cost must be determined. Then a strict shooting schedule must be set up, and each scene must be rehearsed.

3. The film must not oversell. Harping on one theme is always harmful. Get in a basic idea, but keep the "preaching" to a minimum. A good way to do this is to mix entertainment with information. Be certain that even in the title nothing is suggested which may cause the audience to say, "Oh, it's just another movie telling how the schools need money."

4. Select a competent narrator. Remember the importance of a convincing speaker whose voice is pleasant and animated. If possible, someone on your staff should narrate the film. Otherwise, secure a skilled outsider.

5. Introductory comments will "alert" the audience. A brief mimeographed page of opening remarks might be prepared, including the title of the film, some of the highlights of the story, and other interesting facts. But, of course, beware of giving away the story.

Other timely tips:
1. Set up a distribution system.
2. Select an audience which has an impact on public opinion.
3. Determine the number of prints which your city will require.
4. Keep films in good condition.

5. Set up a file of booking confirmations (the date the film is to be shown, the hour, place, occasion, and other information).

6. Have a preview for a group of your community leaders. If your film is good the word will be spread, and requests for showings will come in.

Having proved its effectiveness for many institutions and organizations, the motion picture has become a must in a well-rounded program of public relations. Its impact on the public mind is tremendous and lasting. New uses for films are constantly being discovered. Wise school leaders will no longer be content just to tell the public. They will use motion pictures and other visual aids to *show* the public—to demonstrate their ideas in such a way that they will be unforgettable.

"What will it cost?" That question faces any school administrator. Usually the value exceeds the cost. A cheap visual aid is costly indeed in terms of the misunderstandings which may result. Whatever type you choose, be sure that it is the best, for only the best can bring about the desired audience reaction.

26. *Advertisements That Pull*

ADVERTISING is "salesmanship in print." That means that educational advertisements—both those financed or donated by interested groups and those financed by the schools themselves—must show certain benefits which will come to the community as a result of a plan or proposal.

The most resultful advertising depends on factual, illustrative, and emotional appeals to the reader—to the reader as "you," directly or implied. The viewpoint of the writer should be that of the reader, not that of the school administrator.

In writing effective education copy you must overcome the handicap of distance by intelligence and visualization. In preparing an advertisement, imagine yourself as the prospect and ask, "Just what would make me favor the new high school building proposal?" "Why should I pay more taxes for schools?" "What interest do I have in 'parents' night'?" Your answers will yield ideas and suggestions. Then write in terms of the reader you want to convince. No matter how well you know your program, try to know the reader better.

Keep these suggestions in mind:

1. Select the benefits and appeals.
2. Organize the selling points that support them.
3. Be generous with white space—a crowded advertisement looks unattractive.
4. Use dramatic, eye-catching illustrations.
5. Try to arrest attention quickly without being sensational.
6. Don't overstate, but paint in the best colors you can.
7. Give your layout freedom and movement.
8. Remember that your advertisement is competing for attention with scores of other items (news stories, cartoons, features, illustrations, and so on) in the same issue.
9. Mix facts with emotional appeals. When head and heart are in conflict the heart usually wins.
10. Write enthusiastic copy.
11. Use testimonials from those who mold public opinion in your community.
12. Avoid using too many facts or statistics in a single advertisement.
13. State clearly the benefits which will come from the proposal or program.
14. Emphasize one basic idea.
15. Conclude with a bid for action.

Public relations advertising may be sponsored by the school system, merchants, individuals, or organizations. Local campaigns, designed and directed by community groups, have done much to encourage a broader and more active interest in the schools. Public understanding of the many problems facing modern education has been heightened through the national advertising campaigns designed and promoted by various groups.

Effective advertisements which give special emphasis to the problems faced by schools are prepared and distributed free of charge by the Advertising Council, Inc.[1] The council, a nonprofit, nonpartisan organization, serves the American people by marshaling the forces of advertising to promote volunteer individual action in solving national problems. Proofs of a series of individual advertisements are sent by the council to managers of every daily newspaper in the United States and to the publishers of approximately five thousand major weekly newspapers. Editors are urged to contribute newspaper space as a public service and to persuade local firms, industries, organizations, and individuals to sponsor advertisements. Although the kit containing advertising copy and other material is designed primarily for newspapers, the mats supplied by the council can be used by local printers in making effective handbills and posters.

Activities of the Advertising Council are a part of the "Better Schools Campaign" which is sponsored by the National Citizens Commission for the Public Schools, the United States Office of Education, and the Citizens Federal Committee on Education which includes representatives of business, labor, the National Congress of Parents and Teachers, the American Association of University Women, the General Federation of Women's Clubs, and other leading organizations.

Through newspaper, radio, television, and national magazine and transit advertising, American business and the advertising industry are contributing millions of dollars of advertising space and time in behalf of the nationwide program for better schools.

Display advertisements for local use are made available to individuals and organizations each year by the National Education Association as one method of promoting the annual American Education Week. The N.E.A. also makes available to local groups a great variety of other aids, which include manuals, posters, mats, stickers, plays, bibliographies, motion picture trailers, radio scripts and recordings, stencils, and leaflets.

[1] The council is located at 25 West 45th Street, New York 19, New York.

For the most part, public relations advertising can help the public to understand the philosophies, problems, achievements, and aims of education. At times, copy and art can be combined to correct misconceptions regarding schools and their activities. On other occasions, the public is reminded of the crisis in education and of the need of the support and understanding of the citizens.

As in any phase of public relations, an advertising program should be planned with expert guidance. An attempt must be made to throw light on areas of misunderstanding. Special attention must be given to timing, because it is tremendously important that you say precisely what you want to say to a specific audience at a specific time. Geared to other activities, advertising can be one of the most important members of the public relations family.

27. *Your "Red Letter" Days*

WHAT DO YOU DO when company comes? Do you capitalize on special events and programs? Do your affairs represent the schools in such a way that increased support and cooperation result? Do you take advantage of every opportunity to sponsor special events?

"Any special event is always a lot of trouble. It's just another headache," a superintendent said recently. To be sure, it is a lot of trouble in the sense that a successful event demands extra planning and work. But the dividends will be increased returns in understanding and good will.

Yes, you can sponsor so many extra programs that they lack any degree of interest. Moreover, teachers and students cannot be expected to devote too much time to out-of-the-ordinary programs. The success or failure of a special event is determined by the enthusiasm and interest of those who present it. Indeed, your first task as an administrator is to sell teachers and students on the idea. Once that is done, preparation for the event should get under way.

Here are some pointers for making the most of your special events:

1. Determine the objectives.
2. Decide on the nature of the program.
3. Estimate the prospective attendance and decide on the space needed.
4. Determine the cost.
5. Select the public to be reached.
6. Issue invitations to special guests.
7. Set dates most convenient for the audience.
8. Outline a time schedule of events on the program.
9. Name a planning committee, a chairman, and assistants.
10. Outline detailed assignments.
11. Give directions for follow-up work.
12. Set up a central clearance office.
13. Determine who shall sponsor the program—one class, one school, the system as a whole, the Parent-Teacher Association, or others.
14. Publicize the event in newspapers and school publications, by direct mail, telephone, and by announcements at clubs and meetings.
15. Arrange for posters, photographs, and transit cards.
16. Make plans to handle traffic in the halls.
17. See that there is material for the visitors to take home.
18. Be sure the building is spic and span, and that the temperature is correct.
19. Provide a nursery and a checkroom.
20. See that there are parking lot attendants.
21. Provide special exhibits.
22. If tours of the classrooms are planned, see that work in each room is dramatized for the visitors.
23. Set up an information booth.
24. Provide a system of checking results of the program.
25. Send thank-you letters to all who assisted.
26. Make a scrapbook of the event.
27. Invite suggestions for next year's program.

If too many events are held during the school year, the ultimate result on the part of the public will be indifference toward
the whole program. School leaders must always bear in mind
that not all operations and phases of school life are necessarily
of interest to the public. This means, of course, that the event
should be planned with the public in mind.

A program of this type is hard work. But if it is successful, it is
certain to build understanding.

28. *Annual Reports Come to Life*

TODAY annual reports are regarded as vital cogs in
the school-community public relations machinery. Planning
the report should be the co-operative endeavor of many persons: administrators, teachers, students, laymen, and others.
Items to be considered include (1) the objective, (2) the cost,
(3) the schedule of production, (4) preparation of the material,
(5) the format, and (6) distribution.

Reports vary, of course, in communities. Questions of curious
parents should be answered and misunderstandings should be
cleared up. At the same time, the report is invaluable in point-
ing out the needs and progress of the system. The annual report
should be the year's high spot in the public relations program.

1. Give the publication a catchy title, such as "Our Greatest
Investment," and indicate that it is an annual report in the
subtitle.

2. Know the reader thoroughly.

3. Report fully, clearly, and graphically the activities of the
system for the preceding year.

4. Make the editorial content and physical appearance attractive, accurate, and interesting.

Basic Steps:

1. Appoint a representative group months in advance to begin preparation of the "dummy."

2. Determine the potential readers.

3. Prepare a preliminary outline of the contents, including the main sections and illustrations.

4. Consult a number of outstanding reports from other systems for ideas.

5. Use a check list to determine the content.

6. Select material which presents a balanced outline of the year's work.

FORMAT OF THE REPORT

Cover
Title Page
Foreword
Introductions (by the board of education and the administrative staff)
Table of Contents
Text
  Historical Data
  Activities of the Past Year
    Population growth
    Business services
      accounting and auditing
      financial and statistical requests
      legal procedure
      research
      purchasing procedure
    Plans for school buildings
    Attendance and enrolment
    Health
    Extracurricular activities
    Transportation
    Special services
      advisory placement service
      co-operative programs with community groups
    Legislation
    Professional associations
      publications and research

curricular services
general co-ordination
curriculum laboratory service
audio-visual service
school library service
guidance and special education
Health and physical education
Trade, vocational, and industrial education service
Finances, needs
Objectives (written by the superintendent)
Organizational chart of the complete system

The illustrations may be photographs, drawings, maps, charts, graphs, layouts, and so on. Use pictographs rather than tables of figures. The copy should be interesting, it should be concise, and the language should be simple and vivid.

Distribute the annual report to:
Board of education members
School and city librarians
The entire staff of the school system
Presidents of all civic clubs
Editors of newspapers
All city officials
The Chamber of Commerce
The head of the labor council
Members of the ministerial alliance
YMCA and YWCA libraries
Presidents of the P.T.A. units
Heads of lodges
Other city superintendents
Deans of education in universities
The state department of instruction
Parents
Presidents of study clubs

Publicity:
Hold a conference for press and radio representatives, describing the highlights of the report. Ask administrative work-

ers and principals to present portions of the report at faculty meetings, and encourage teachers and all staff members to study it. Recommend that the P.T.A. devote a meeting to it, and suggest to civics teachers that they use the report in classes.

No aspect of school administration offers superintendents greater opportunity to demonstrate leadership, win friends, and get ideas across to the public than an attractive annual report. Be certain that your story is humanized, that it is understandable and interesting. Don't allow your report to be handicapped by tradition. Find something unique in your program; interpret the year's operations in such a way that they can be tied into a central theme. As a result you will get readership—and action.

29. *Newsletters Can Be Readable, Too*

IN THESE TIMES the school superintendent must be a superman. Each day he faces enough problems to exhaust the average man. To be successful, he must keep in touch with his staff—teachers, principals, custodians, office workers, bus drivers—in fact, with everyone who is employed by the board of education.

Now he can't always find time for personal visits. But he can maintain contacts through a regular newsletter, a combination of news items and capsules of wisdom and inspiration. If messages are to be read, they must be short, snappy, and to the point. No preaching. No long editorials. Just a lot of small items told in a conversational style.

Check your newsletter or bulletin for these items:
1. changes in policies.
2. new classes.
3. new equipment.
4. short reprints from other publications.
5. figures on enrollment.
6. new teaching aids.

116

7. the financial program.

8. activities of administrators and principals.

9. changes in personnel.

10. inspiration and practical advice on personality improvement.

11. coming meetings and events.

12. praise from parents and others on work well done

13. quotations from letters praising schools, services, or activities.

14. roundup of items of interest from other schools.

15. pictures and biographies of old-timers in the system.

16. technical information (readable) about new buildings or facilities.

17. honors and awards which have come to staff members.

18. "pet peeves" of custodians (cleverly done, this can be most effective).

19. news notes of former administrators.

20. news of citations to system or individual schools.

Here are some suggestions to help make your newsletter successful:

1. Establish a unique format so that readers can readily identify your publication.

2. Write "you" and talk "you." Show your staff members how they can benefit by following your suggestions, not how the suggestions will help you as an administrator.

3. Give praise and inspiration in easy-to-take doses.

4. Invite contributions from your associates and teachers.

5. Freshen old material by giving it a new twist.

6. Make it known that the material in your newsletter is exclusive and not available elsewhere.

7. Avoid comparisons that may cause embarrassment, resentment, or discouragement.

8. Write from your own experience.

9. See that the appearance of the bulletin (including the headlines, make-up, illustrations, and printing) is attractive.

10. Be on the alert for ideas from similar publications.

Do not dull the effect of the newsletter with an overdose of announcements. Aside from official notices, it should contain a variety of information, including humorous and inspirational items. In the words of one superintendent: "My newsletter is my regular contact with the whole school 'family' so I try to give it the attention it deserves."

30. *When You Must Speak*

IF YOU WANT to influence people, if you want to gain wider acceptance for your ideas, then the speech—the effective speech—is a potent good will builder.

Too many superintendents sound like their financial reports; too many teachers talk to adults on the classroom level. The spoken word is still a mighty tool. Rightly used by administrators and teachers, it will send your public-approval curve climbing.

Here are some tips from some of the nation's best speakers:
1. Say something which will break through your listeners' initial apathy.
2. Keep to the point.
3. Talk in terms of your listeners' experiences and interests.
4. Keep your speech marching toward a very definite goal.
5. Make use of conversational phrases such as, "Now haven't you often wished that—?"
6. Maintain an alert body carriage.
7. Look at your audience.
8. Speak sincerely, spontaneously, and directly in an animated voice.
9. In every way make the listeners feel that you are one of them.
10. Do not let your appearance steal the show.
11. Eliminate distressing mannerisms.
12. Do not be surprised at interruptions.

13. Find out in advance the purpose of the organization to which you are speaking, its achievements, its services, and its ideals.

14. Never apologize for the time you are taking or mention the time allotted to you. If your information is worth while, you have no need to apologize.

15. Avoid trying to cover too much in one talk.

16. Be sure that the audience can see you.

17. Never attempt to bluff an audience. It won't work.

18. Employ a change of pace in the presentation of material: use an anecdote, quote a nationally-known authority, or run in a story to illustrate your point.

19. Use visual aids whenever possible.

Let us say that you plan to hold a meeting. Have you made an agenda, or do you intend to speak from a few scrawled notes on the back of an envelope? Did you analyze your last meeting to see why it succeeded or failed? A meeting can accomplish a good deal, and it can keep those in attendance interested. Check these factors before planning your next meeting and then watch for results.

Start with a clear conception of the purpose. Considerations include:

1. Means by which the objective can be attained.

2. Misunderstandings regarding the present program or practices.

3. Persons to be influenced, their attitudes and convictions.

4. The job to be done and the necessity for effective performance by all concerned.

5. The timing. Psychologically, it is wise to hold a meeting at a time when those in attendance can get on the job and apply the inspiration and information which they have received.

Have a continuing meeting structure:

1. Specific planning and preparation are always necessary.

2. Material and ideas must be collected.

3. The leader must be on the alert for workable ideas from other groups.

4. Periodic conferences of small groups permit co-ordination within the larger group.

5. As soon as one meeting is out of the way, begin plans for the next one, and in this way avoid the feverish, last-minute, ineffective gathering.

Plan the presentation:

1. Is it to be an inspirational meeting, an analysis of the present program, a discussion of over-all problems? Are new ideas to be introduced, or is the meeting designed as a refresher session?

2. Establish a few definite objectives which are attainable.

3. Have a timely theme.

4. Operate on a set time schedule (inform each speaker in advance exactly how many minutes he is allowed to speak).

5. Use showmanship if it ties in with the educational purpose of the meeting.

6. Make full use of effective visual aids.

7. Keep the meeting on a plane of informality.

8. Encourage the participation of many people, and see that each contributes to the main objective.

9. Summarize the highlights of the meeting.

10. See that each person knows exactly what he is to do when he returns to his work after the meeting.

11. Provide each person with material he can take with him.

12. End the session on a strong achievement note.

Thou shalt not:

1. Call a meeting to make a lot of announcements (unless the emergency is great).

2. Plan a meeting filled with pep talks (teachers resent this).

So You're the Chairman!

You have just attended a meeting that was a flop. Why? It had great possibilities of informing or persuading those in attendance. The speaker was fairly good, but something was lacking. It just didn't click. What was wrong? Merely this: no definite technique was followed in planning or conducting the meeting.

Here are suggestions which will help you do a better job:

1. Plan your program in advance.

2. Put your plans in writing with a schedule showing time allotted to each portion of the meeting.

3. Arrange for an auditorium or dining room far in advance.

4. Think in terms of a unique presentation—a program that people won't want to miss.

5. Get the best talent available. Ask your friends to tell you of interesting speakers they have heard.

6. Be on duty long before the program starts. Check the ventilation and temperature of the room, see that the public address system is ready and that the speaker's stand is in place. If movies are to be shown, arrange for someone to turn off the house lights.

7. You are the host. Meet your speaker or have someone meet him when he arrives in town, and see that he gets to his hotel room. Allow him plenty of free time. He probably isn't interested in your new boiler or playground equipment—he might choose to write letters, go over his lectures notes, or just take it easy in his room. Make arrangements for someone to pick him up at the hotel if you cannot do so. At the meeting introduce him to officers and guests at the head table and wait until the program has ended to introduce him to other guests.

8. You run the show. As master of ceremonies you must be enthusiastic. You must make your introduction brief, complete, and lively. You must know your speaker's name, how it is pronounced, his title or position. Avoid trite phrases such as "a man who needs no introduction." Dick Borden says that the speech of introduction answers these questions: Why this subject? Why this subject before this audience? Why this subject before this audience at this time? Why this subject before this audience at this time by this speaker? Rise to a climax in the

introduction, but above all, do not steal the spotlight from the guest speaker.

Panel Discussions

Americans have never lacked for something to talk about. From the town meetings of early times to the round-table conferences of today, they have made a habit of getting together to talk about topics of interest. Panel discussions are being used to a greater degree to close the gaps between school and community. They are of immense value to administrators and teachers in sampling public opinion and in getting excellent advice from laymen. By this method citizens feel that they are sharing as partners.

Make the most of your panel by following these suggestions:

1. When you invite people to appear, tell them the topic, the exact time of the meeting, the location, and the purpose of the affair.

2. Introduce everyone present.

3. Seat your speakers so that each member of the group can be seen by the rest and by the audience.

4. Start on time.

5. At the beginning of the meeting explain the topic briefly, its importance, and its timeliness.

6. Keep the meeting as informal as possible.

7. Avoid making a speech yourself and don't allow anyone else to make one.

8. Limit each speaker to two minutes and see that each one is given an opportunity to voice his opinions.

9. Keep the discussion on the track.

10. Have "starter" questions ready if the pace slows down.

11. Keep the discussion on a friendly plane.

12. Save about ten minutes to sum up the views and suggestions presented during the discussion. Be as fair and accurate as you can.

13. Thank members of the audience for their questions and interest, and thank the speakers for their contributions.

14. Stop on time.

31. *Making Friends by Telephone*

THE TELEPHONE can be a mighty tool in public relations. If you would have a good telephone personality, first be sure that you are easy to understand, then seek to make the pleasant impression that will bring a friendly response. Always put yourself in the other person's shoes. Be courteous. Don't interrupt, argue, or be impatient. Suppose the other person is upset or angry about something that has gone wrong. Here is a chance to make or lose a friend. Express regret and apologize if necessary. Good will can be won or lost by telephone, and often we fumble our opportunities to make a good impression. Check on your telephone habits:

1. Do you answer the phone before the third ring?
2. Do you identify yourself when you answer?
3. Do you talk with a pencil, cigar, or pipe in your mouth?
4. Do you speak in a natural tone directly into the mouthpiece?
5. Do you make an effort to make your voice sound pleasing, that is, are you courteous rather than curt or indifferent?
6. Do you ask necessary questions politely?
7. Do you keep a pad and pencil handy so you won't have to hunt for them when the conversation starts?
8. Do you courteously ask the other party to hold the line when you leave the telephone to obtain information?
9. Do you thank the other party for waiting when you return?
10. Do you offer to call back in cases where it requires some time to secure the necessary information?
11. Do you offer to take a message or the telephone number when the call is not for you?
12. Do you arrange to have someone answer your telephone when you are away from your office or desk?
13. Do you say good-by or otherwise definitely close your conversation?

14. Do you wait for the calling party to hang up first?
15. Do you always replace the receiver gently?

Hundreds of persons make telephone calls to schools daily. What impression do they receive? All persons who talk regularly from schools—office workers, principals, clerks, students, cafeteria managers, bus drivers, and others—should be reminded that by following simple rules of courtesy they can make pleasant impressions.

32. *School Buildings Tell the Story*

UNLIKE many phases of public relations, the school plant of the community is tangible and concrete. It stands day and night as physical evidence of an ideal. It should make positive impressions on visitors and passers-by.

Public pride in school buildings and grounds is easy to obtain. Attractive plants are looked upon as community assets by the citizens. If funds are insufficient for maintenance and operation, that fact should be emphasized by the superintendent. Whatever the amount of funds allocated for maintenance, the administrator should do everything possible to see that buildings are kept in excellent condition at all times.

Building check list
1. Is all equipment kept in repair?
2. Is the ventilation system adequate?
3. Is the temperature always correct?
4. Are the acoustics good?
5. Are the interior and exterior colors pleasant and effective?
6. Are the rooms lighted correctly?
7. Is every room planned for comfort, utility, and convenience?
8. Do the buildings meet the standards of the best construction in the community?

Here are some suggestions to aid in the improvement of the school buildings:

1. Use spotlights for decorative lighting.
2. See that custodians and helpers are carefully trained and supervised.
3. Recognize the fact that a well-kept school, now subject to use many hours of the day, requires more workers.
4. See that the buildings are spic-and-span before special events (floors and foyers polished, walls brushed, vitreous ware cleaned, and marks and defacing removed).
5. See that the custodians have the best equipment and supplies available.
6. Make sure that the buildings are always clean and sanitary.
7. See that fire escapes, fire extinguishers, pressure bars on outside doors, safety screens, and all other protective devices are inspected at regular intervals.

School Grounds

1. Have playground equipment checked regularly.
2. Provide parking areas for teachers and patrons.
3. Keep the lawns, flower beds, shrubs, and walks attractive.
4. Have the lawns and schoolyards designed by a landscape architect.
5. Change the arrangement of flowers from year to year.
6. See that every precaution for safety is taken, both in the building and on the grounds.

What lies ahead? That is the major question of the superintendent in planning improvements for his schools. He must consider the adequacy of present buildings, future requirements, the kind of community the school plant is to serve, and the needs of both the youths and the adults of the town.

Furthermore, the superintendent must always consider such building essentials as a good foundation, a durable roof, strong, tight walls, and adequate exits. Other factors he must consider are modern lighting (both artificial and natural), adequate ventilation, modern heating, ample storage space, work alcoves, built-ins, and facilities for audio-visual education. Special attention must be given to the design of rooms used for handicrafts, dramatics, industrial arts, science, and other subjects which require special classroom facilities.

Today more and more schools are designed and constructed with multiple areas, radiant heating, attractive color schemes, movable partitions, and other modern features. Buildings are now being constructed to meet the needs of the students.

With the public as a partner in planning, the needs for new buildings are easier to interpret. "You know, I learned a long time ago that if I let the public help me in plans for a school plant I could move faster," a superintendent commented. "You see, it isn't enough that a need exist for a new building; that need must also exist in the minds of the citizens."

Practically any medium may be used to explain the needs for new equipment. Present equipment may be outmoded, limited, and costly to operate because of its age and condition. Publicity campaigns for new supplies should be organized with care. Every step should be planned and analyzed. Present facilities may be out-of-date, inadequate, uneconomical to operate, unsuited to new conditions, unsanitary, beyond repair, or unsafe. Appeals should be made in a positive tone, and these appeals should stress the need, the method of installing and maintaining the new equipment economically, its time and space saving advantages, its durability, appearance, and so on.

The role of the school plant is unending. It is easy to see that the public will pay for and be proud of buildings that are attractive, practical, and well equipped. Grooming of the school plant is a must in the task of building good will.

33. *Successful Publicity*

EDUCATION is one of the biggest news stories in the nation. But whether or not newspapers will carry that story is determined by many elements, both tangible and intangible.

Perhaps your next door neighbor is aware that education has become a giant enterprise, but he may have only the haziest notions regarding its aims, problems, and activities. In general, the mass of people are still uninformed about the real values of education.

Much has been said about the power of the press. Critics have launched many attacks on the modern newspaper; yet it is still the principal medium of communication for the distribution of news and opinions to large groups of people. We must use the press in telling our story to the public.

Editors obtain school news in two ways:

1. by assigning their reporters to cover the schools and

2. by receiving news which is written by a staff member or worker associated with the school system.

You already have some ideas for bettering your relations with editors and reporters. But you say, "We must write our own news." That's fine. First of all, learn all you can about newspaper production. Learn to understand the problems of editors. Take a course in journalism, if possible, or read some good books on reporting. Editors don't expect school workers to be expert writers, but those assigned the task of reporting school news should know the basic essentials of journalistic style.

In writing news stories keep these rules in mind: (1) state facts only, not personal opinions; (2) tell your story briefly, in simple language, then stop; (3) answer the questions who, what, where, when, and why early in the story; (4) make the report accurate and coherent; (5) paragraph and punctuate properly; (6) be especially careful about names, titles, hours, and subjects; (7) avoid abbreviations, slang, adjectives, wordiness, and involved sentences; (8) omit headlines; (9) submit clean typewritten copy, double-spaced; and (10) always get your story in on time.

Make the first few words count. Give all the facts in a brief fashion. Make the opening paragraph, called the "lead" (pronounced "leed"), one that gets attention.

Notice the variety in the following leads:

WHO: James G. Smith, superintendent of the Blankville public schools, has been named a member of the state education survey committee—

WHAT: One school bus was condemned and two more sent to garages for repairs following the annual inspection—

WHY: Because he was the leader of a gang which broke into Carrel Junior High School Hallowe'en night, Fred Kastner, fifteen years old, had to explain to Judge Blank—

WHERE: The principal's office at Horace Mann Junior High School was the scene today of—

WHEN: September 2 has been designated by school officials as the final date on which parents can enroll their children—

HOW: After winning first place in the state oratorical contest held in Blankville, John Smith, Webster high senior, was named—

CONDITIONAL CLAUSE: Because Lucille Jones, fifteen-year-old high school girl, was not permitted to have dates, she ran away from home, she admitted when found today by—

SUBSTANTIVE CLAUSE: That more than half of the school buildings in Blankville need immediate repairs is the warning contained in the monthly report made today by—

PUNCH: The school custodians strike has ended.

CARTRIDGE: School is out! Thousands of yelling youngsters—

ASTONISHER: The largest school bond issue in the history of Blankville will be decided by voters—

PREPOSITIONAL PHRASE: Despite their heavy teaching loads, faculty members of Blankville high school found time to write thirty-four magazine articles during the past school year.

DIRECT QUOTATION: "Americans do not yet have schools for children—we have schools for adults," Dr. E. K. Wilson of State University told those attending the annual education conference here today.

INDIRECT QUOTATION: No community in America ever had a better school system than it wanted, according to Paul Cooper, president of the Kentucky Education Association—

SITUATION: In the same room where he began his education at the Judson school, Roy K. Heron formally became superintendent of schools in a brief ceremony.

QUESTION: Should students be permitted to grade teachers?

CROWDED: Standing committees were appointed, twelve new teachers were named, the football field lighting contract was renewed for another year, salaries of dieticians were raised, and the annual report of the superintendent of schools was approved at the monthly meeting of the board of education Tuesday night. (In general, avoid this type of lead.)

DIRECT ADDRESS: You have heard the old gag about the only way some people get out of school is when woodpeckers eat the building. Well, it almost happened at Denver Consolidated—

HUMAN INTEREST: All the bad luck that could befall one unhappy man has tumbled down on Jim Atkins, custodian at Blankville High School.

PICTURE: Smeared with mud, wet and chilled, ten-year-old Robert Kerr today told police about a 300-mile ride on the spare tire of an overland bus.

CONTRAST: Twenty-five years ago Tony Morgan was a high school kid who begged his chemistry instructor to let him do extra experiments after school hours. Tuesday he was elected president of the American Chemical Society at its annual meeting in Seattle.

PARTICIPIAL: Burned Friday when a boiler exploded at Lincoln School, Gordon Melvin, fifty-six, custodian, 1856 Elm Street, died Saturday afternoon in Municipal hospital.

INFINITIVE PHRASE: To call the public's attention to the opening of American Education Week, students of Overstreet High School, led by the school band, will parade down Main Street at 3:30 Friday afternoon.

LITERARY ALLUSION: Horace Greeley's admonition to "go west, young man, go west" apparently still has its lure for two Denver youths, even though the pioneering days of the great wide open spaces may be a thing of the past.

SUSPENDED INTEREST: School officials are on the lookout for a former teacher named Jones today. It is a complicated story.

EPIGRAM: He who laughs last laughs best, the books say.

SUMMARY: John Ferguson, former superintendent of schools in Blankville, now dean of education at State Teachers College, disclosed Tuesday that he has accepted the presidency of State University effective next year.

PARODY: Daniel J. Norton fiddles while Miami burns. The seventy-eight-year-old former music teacher, who lives at 3423 Elmwood, believes fiddling is the best way to beat the heat.

SEQUENCE: Billy Smith, student at Horace Mann Junior High School, left home to catch the school bus as usual at 7:45 this morning.

CRUSADE OR POLICY: Fourteen more teachers resigned Thursday from the Putnam Center school system. The week's total resignations is twenty-seven, Superintendent George Beckman reported Thursday night.

FIGURATIVE: A discordant note sounded yesterday in the musical ambitions of two Jonesville High School students.

PITFALLS TO BE AVOIDED IN PUBLICITY COPY[1]

1. Failure to follow correct newspaper style.
2. Poor appearance of copy.
3. Trivial event.
4. Too many superlatives.
5. Padded story.
6. Poor timing.
7. Failure to distinguish between news and advertising.
8. Failure to indicate that story is exclusive.
9. Lack of local interest.
10. Unsuitability for newspaper.
11. "Heavy" information.
12. Story lacking pep.
13. Failure to include art.
14. Incompleteness.
15. Failure to meet deadline.
16. Lack of "You" approach.

[1] Adapted from Harral, *Patterns of Publicity Copy* (Norman, University of Oklahoma Press, 1950), 23–30.

17. Propagandizing.
18. Suggesting position, length, and headline for story.
19. One-sided presentation.
20. Use of scientific and technical terms, academic language, essay form.
21. Lack of interpretation.
22. Editorializing.
23. Favoritism in distribution.
24. Inaccuracy, use of rumors.
25. Poor punctuation.
26. Use of slang and abbreviations.
27. Incoherence.
28. Buried lead.
29. Misquotation.
30. Omission of source of news and reporter.
31. Limited news value.
32. Request that story be printed as a "favor."

Appearance of Copy

1. See that the copy is neatly typed (on one side of the paper only), double or triple spaced, with ample margins on all sides.
2. Give the source of the news (the name of the writer, school, address, and telephone number).
3. If the release is more than one page long, number the pages.
4. If a special release date is requested, indicate at the top of the copy.

Study newspapers critically—know what makes the stories click. Cultivate the ability to seek out news. Analyze the things you see and hear in terms of possible stories. Always remember that newspaper copy should be easy to read. Any word or phrase that derails the train of thought decreases the readability of the story. People read newspapers hurriedly. They have no time to consult a dictionary when they run across unusual words. This means that you must omit such words and phrases as "enriched curriculum," "core content," "distributive education," and others which are not in general use outside the profession. The more your story conforms to the style and pattern of material used by newspapers, the higher your placement of publicity will be.

The Publicity Campaign

Superintendent K's publicity program was the type other administrators dreamed about. He had no full-time public relations workers, yet his school system was high in the public's favor. His system was no richer in news possibilities than scores of others, yet feature stories about his schools were often seen in professional journals. Even the state press regularly carried items about his programs. His achievements were usually dismissed with one word—luck.

Then one day at a regional education meeting he was asked the secret of his success as a publicist. He replied, "There isn't any secret to it. We plan our publicity, that's all."

That settled one important question, but it left another unanswered. What is planned publicity? It is an awareness of news values plus a long-range plan of interpretation. It is careful timing and the ability to make the most of every newsworthy event and situation. It is the realization that news of education must be spaced (providing it isn't spot news which must be released immediately) so that the campaign has continuity and interest.

Here are some factors to keep in mind when planning a publicity campaign:

1. Get the facts on the situation.

2. Determine whom you want to influence.

3. Combine what you want to present with what the people want to know.

4. List the objectives, then review them and make any changes necessary.

5. Make a schedule of stories which can be developed from the situation.

6. Seek ideas from similar situations in other communities for your own campaign.

7. Plan different types of stories: interviews, quotations from speeches, straight news, and features.

8. Select the channels which will be most resultful.

9. Run over the list of stories for picture possibilities.

10. Tie in newspaper publicity with direct mail, school literature, and other channels.

11. Provide a budget to cover all expenses.

12. Plan the campaign so that it is neither too long nor too short.

13. Be prepared for any unforeseen change in plans.

14. Make full use of leaders to inform and influence others.

15. Remember that news stories must be *news*.

16. Invite newspapermen and representatives of radio stations, advertising agencies, and direct-mail companies to serve as members of your committee.

17. Avoid, as much as possible, launching your campaign at a time when others are in progress in your community.

18. Emphasize the most interesting, the most dramatic, and the most newsworthy phases of your campaign.

19. In literature, stories, and broadcasts, make full use of testimonials and statements from community leaders.

20. Select an apt theme or slogan around which to build the campaign.

21. Check on the results of previous drives and profit by the procedures which have been utilized.

22. Take time—plenty of time—to plan the program.

A News Arithmetic to Show You When a Story Is News

1 ordinary student plus ordinary grades=0
1 ordinary student plus 12 years' perfect attendance=NEWS
1 ordinary high school principal plus 1 ordinary wife=0
1 ordinary high school principal plus 3 wives=NEWS
1 school board treasurer plus 1 wife plus 2 children=0
1 school board treasurer minus $12,000=NEWS
1 ordinary teacher plus daily routine=0
1 teacher plus new way of teaching subject=NEWS

1 ordinary home economics class plus usual grades=0

1 home economics class plus 1 boy who makes highest grades=NEWS

1 ordinary student plus routine job after hours=0

1 student plus job selling goldfish after school and on Saturdays=NEWS

1 ordinary high school student plus 4 years of study=0

1 high school student plus extreme poverty plus physical infirmity plus distinction in scholarship=NEWS

1 ordinary teacher plus Christmas party=0

1 teacher plus Christmas party held in her honor by 150 former students=NEWS

1 ordinary school bus plus hundreds of miles of travel each year=0

1 school bus plus driver's failure to stop at railroad crossing=NEWS

1 ordinary report card plus usual comments plus usual parent's signature=0

1 report card plus teacher's comment, "Betty is a fine student but she talks too much," plus father's signature plus his comment, "You should come by sometime and meet her mother."= NEWS

1 ordinary group of teachers plus extra work in helping in community enterprises=0

1 group of teachers plus annual report showing wide variety of services in extracurricular affairs plus number of hours given to work=NEWS

34. *When the Reporter Calls*

MANY FACTORS are involved in profitable press relations, among them a knowledge of news values, newspaper make-up, reader interest, news patterns, and circulation.

The reporter has three functions: (1) he must gather the facts, (2) he must write the story, and (3) he must get the story into the office in time for publication.

Tips for effective press relations:

1. Play fair with newspapers if you expect them to play fair with you.

2. Establish personal contacts with members of the newspaper staff.

3. Lose no opportunity to be of service to reporters and editors.

4. Do not send an editor thinly veiled school propaganda or advertising.

5. Since newspapers attempt to mirror life, do not expect them to publish only the stories that are favorable to schools.

6. Newspaper space is valuable. Don't expect too much space to be devoted to news of education.

7. Evaluate your news through the eyes of the editor.

8. Never be too busy to see a reporter.

9. Don't play favorites. Treat all reporters alike.

10. Be as eager to help the reporter to get the details of an adverse story as you would a favorable one.

11. If an editor has been generous in giving space to news of school affairs, don't strain your relationship by continually demanding more.

12. Express your appreciation to reporters and editors.

13. Invite representatives of the press to banquets, receptions, or special occasions.

14. Do not evade or side-step a reporter's questions. He may think you have something to hide.

15. Remember that a reporter seeks facts, not hearsay or rumor.

16. Don't be condescending. Reporters deal with all types of people.

17. Plan for dull days by having several tips for feature stories.

18. Don't ask the reporter for favors. He isn't the editor.

19. Don't expect the impossible. Trust the editor to know news values.

20. Keep an idea file of potential news stories, features, and pictures.

WHEN YOU DON'T KNOW

There comes a time when the reporter will ask questions you can't answer. It's bound to happen. The reporter has run across the situation many times before, so there's no reason to evade the question. Admit that you don't know and then be as helpful as you can. Call someone in your system who might know. Check your files carefully and get in touch with the person who may have been the source of such news in the past. In short, make every effort to be of service. If the information isn't available at the time, take advantage of the opportunity to make a friend. When the data for the reporter does become available —even though it may be several days or even weeks later—let him know at once. You may think it is too late to do him any good, but let the reporter decide that. By doing this, you will establish yourself as a person of your word. In all cases, answer the query as soon as possible.

35. *Students Write the Headlines*

OFTEN AN ADMINISTRATOR overlooks the importance of student publications in his interpretative program. He is likely to minimize the importance of these channels—the student newspaper, yearbook, handbook, and other publications— in reaching a most important segment of his public. As an instrument of good will, each medium has enormous possibilities (1) because it has extremely high readership value and (2) because it reaches practically every student.

Administrators, teachers, and sponsors should be frank in their relationships with staff members of student publications. Any attempt to "cross them up" by devious methods usually has harmful reactions. Frequent meetings between staff members and sponsors will result in better understanding for all. One successful superintendent entertains faculty sponsors and staff members of student publications at a dinner once each semester.

The main problem, perhaps, in making student publications do the greatest possible good in the public relations program is to awaken staff members to the fact that their work will aid the progress of the school. When the importance of their work is pointed out, they are usually co-operative and eager to do all they can in building favorable public opinion.

The student newspaper will

1. reflect the life and activities of the school.
2. afford experience for students interested in journalism.
3. educate students and parents to the school's resources and needs.
4. promote community spirit and interest.
5. unite students and parents in co-operative projects.

Organization of the Newspaper

I. Staff:

1. Assign specific duties to each staff member and see that he understands them.
2. Provide students with close supervision and guidance.
3. Impress on staff members the importance of their work and its potential impact on public opinoin.
4. Instruct the sponsor to name students to both major and minor staff positions.
5. See that experience in minor positions is a prerequisite for major positions.

II. Business management:

Most high school newspapers are financed from two main sources of revenues, advertising and circulation. Many, however, are being financed through a subsidy from the school board. Here are some suggestions for conducting a subscription campaign:

1. Set up subscription rates for a semester or year rather than for one or two months.
2. Conduct a contest among school clubs and organizations.
3. See that all who help in the campaign (teachers, staff

members, student leaders) are fully acquainted with selling points.

4. Plan a short, concentrated campaign.

5. Use posters, letters, circulars, exhibits, and announcements at assemblies to advertise the newspaper.

6. Insist that all those working on the campaign submit periodic reports to the sponsor.

7. Hold a follow-up campaign at the beginning of the succeeding semester to contact new students.

III. News standards:

1. See that news coverage presents a balanced picture of school life.

2. Make the stories accurate, timely, interesting, and objective.

3. Encourage wholehearted co-operation between staff members and the adviser who represents the administration.

ELEMENTS OF A SUCCESSFUL YEARBOOK

What are the requirements for a successful yearbook? This will depend, of course, on the type of book you wish to publish. Some are gay, some are sober, and, tragically enough, many look just exactly like hundreds of others.

The yearbook must mirror the school—it must be a realistic picture of life at that particular school. This means that it must be representative of all interests. Good photographs and well-written copy will strengthen a book. Be sure that copy fits space requirements exactly, and remember that original copy will give any book a lift. All photographs should be identified. Unidentified pictures are worse than none at all.

What are the duties of the editor? He must (1) estimate the budget (with the help of the business manager and sponsor), (2) select and supervise the work of editorial assistants, (3) plan the book (its theme, sections, and layouts), (4) obtain pictures, (5) order engravings, (6) write and edit copy, and (7) plan a production schedule that will insure delivery of the annual on time.

Since the editor and the business manager often work hand in hand, it is difficult to list their specific responsibilities and duties. Usually the editor is the production manager and the business manager is in charge of circulation and finance.

General duties of the business manager can be summarized as follows: (1) estimating the budget (with the editor), (2) letting contracts (with the editor and sponsor), (3) selling advertising and preparing it for the printer, (4) conducting the sales campaign, (5) delegating and supervising the work of the business assistants, and (6) distributing the annual.

Remember that a yearbook is seldom thrown away. The sponsor and the student staff members must be satisfied only with the best.

Student Handbooks

A student handbook can be an excellent medium for orienting new students and making them feel that they "belong." If well edited, it will answer their questions about the regulations, activities, and traditions of the school. Because of the many topics which must be covered, space will be at a premium. Therefore the writing must be kept "tight."

Among the topics to be included are:

1. A welcome from the superintendent or principal.
2. A welcome from the president of the student council.
3. Schedules of athletic events.
4. The history and traditions of the school.
5. The year's calendar.
6. The grading system.
7. School songs and cheers.
8. Clubs and organizations.
9. The constitution of the student council.
10. Advisers.
11. Assemblies.
12. Health service.
13. School publications.
14. Student employment.
15. Social regulations.

36. *What About Exhibits?*

REMEMBER when schools confined their exhibits to a few dusty trophies almost hidden in darkened cases in the halls? Not so, today. In these fast-moving, publicity-conscious, promotion-selling days, the ancient art of exposing articles for public view has at last been brought up to date.

Effective exhibits pay dividends. Through careful selection and intelligent planning, more schools are using exhibits as an excellent means of widening their circle of friends. They have proved time and time again that there is no surer, quicker way to correct misconceptions and to create favorable public opinion.

Many exhibits are held with little or no planning, designed on a hit-or-miss basis—that often misses. There is no mystery about the success of some exhibits and the failure of others. Generally speaking, there are only a few basic rules for you to follow. Keep these in mind and you're well on the way to a successful showing. Remember, first of all, that a profitable presentation is a planned presentation. Decide on the principal impression you want to create or the main thought you want to impart. Ask yourself:

1. Do I want to interest parents?
2. Do I want to get over an idea to the public at large?
3. Do I want to correct a misconception?
4. Do I want to show the value of the school program?
5. Do I want to show that students like their schools?
6. Do I want to demonstrate the growth of the school population?
7. Do I want to suggest a needed change in the program?
8. Do I want to show the expenditures for teaching materials?

Then decide what medium you wish to use:

1.	cartoons	7.	slides
2.	posters	8.	sketches
3.	photographs	9.	motion pictures
4.	charts		(sound or silent)
5.	diagrams	10.	dioramas
6.	legends	11.	models

For best results, an exhibit should combine several types of media. As a simple illustration, you could use an enlarged photograph of a school building in the background with charts and models in the foreground. The more universal the appeal, the more effective the exhibit will be. Sometimes this means associating ideas or creating dramatic action. Steel, brick, and mortar for a new building aren't very interesting; but the children who need the structure have a strong appeal.

Exhibits should be located where they are easily accessible. You may have a supercolossal display on the third floor of the high school, but human inertia being what it is (not considering the handicapped, the elderly, and others who couldn't climb the stairs), few people will make any effort to see it. Ordinarily, an exhibit placed near the entrance is seen by more people than one placed farther down the hall.

You must have something compelling in your exhibit to stop the person passing by and to cause him to turn for a second look. You must use showmanship—human interest, drama, light, color, and sound. If exhibits are to contribute to public knowledge concerning education, they should be designed by someone who has experience and talent in this direction. Often teachers who know little about planning exhibits are asked to do such work. Unless they are alert to modern procedures, they are likely to ignore showmanship and their results will be very dull. The old idea that education and drama cannot be combined has been thrown overboard.

Explanatory matter for the exhibit should be written in the language of the public, not in that of an educator. It should be accurate, interesting, and compact. This same suggestion applies to any printed or mimeographed material distributed as a part of the display.

If you are planning an exhibit which is to be shown at several places, be sure to consider the problem of crating it (not always necessary unless shipped by express or freight) so that it can be taken down and reassembled quickly. If your exhibit is being shown with others representing different organizations and institutions at a community affair, find out in advance what you can about competitive activities. Then give yours such an appealing quality that passers-by will stop to learn more. Sometimes it's wise to have an attendant ask visitors to fill out slips. Their names can be used as a mailing list for future publications.

Work as many dramatic and compelling angles into your exhibit as possible. People walking by will either say, "Ho hum, just another exhibit about schools," or they will exclaim, "Say, what's this? Let's see what this is all about!"

Always give consideration to these fundamental factors: (1) objectives, (2) media, (3) appeals, (4) simplicity, and (5) location. Because they convey ideas so quickly and dramatically, exhibits are of increasing importance in the task of interpreting the modern school.

37. *Seeing Is Believing*

THERE ARE few better educational tools than photography. Pictures tell a story, arouse curiosity, and compel reading of the accompanying text. They interpret, dramatize, inform, explain, and entertain. Today photographs are telling more and more of the school's story. Annual reports, for example, no longer consist merely of dreary-looking pages of type and figures. Most current reports allow pictures to tell 80 per cent of the story.

Here are the qualities that make a picture effective:
1. good composition

2. unusual angles
3. clarity of meaning
4. human interest
5. action
6. correct lighting
7. effective background
8. natural pose
9. exact focus
10. dramatic quality

Here are some suggestions for making the most of your relations with the newspaper photographer:

1. Extend him every possible courtesy.

2. Have everything prepared for his visit: the group ready to pose, necessary background material, special lighting arrangements, and so on.

3. Make an outline of possible shots, then allow the photographer to choose from them or use one of his own.

4. Tip off the photographer on possible shots at a forthcoming event.

5. Use tact in preventing the photographer from making undesirable shots.

6. Remember that the city editor, not the photographer, will determine whether the picture will be used.

7. Never ask the photographer for prints of pictures he has taken. His equipment and material are paid for by his newspaper.

8. Make it clear to your personnel that they are to co-operate fully with the photographer.

9. Never be too busy to see a photographer.

10. Evaluate your photographs through the eyes of the newspaper editor.

11. Respect the photographer's wishes, especially on technical matters.

12. Write a note of thanks to a photographer who has done an exceptionally fine job for the schools.

Where can you get ideas for pictures? The best way is to set up a file of effective photographs clipped from newspapers, magazines, journals, promotion literature, and direct mail advertising material. In this way you will get ideas for local use and you will also develop picture-sense. Be sure that your picture tells a story. Use photographs in your newspaper publicity and in your publications. They will be seen—and remembered.

38. *Performance Is the Payoff*

IN EDUCATION, long-term public relations programs seem to excel in one all-important qualification: the ability of administrators to check constantly on the results of their programs—to keep tab on all phases of their informative and interpretative contacts. Sometimes, of course, this habit of checking on performance indicates a need for change. Often it reaffirms the effectiveness of existing methods and procedures. But always it provides a sound current basis for administrative decisions.

Suppose each of us were asked to list the basic factors a program must have to succeed. I doubt if your list and mine, except for certain basic points, would be the same. This isn't surprising. Certain standards are followed in most systems, yet each situation has unique problems which call for specific procedures. The check list presented here is not meant to be all-inclusive. Parts of it may seem dull and innocuous. Nevertheless, when this scale is applied to any program it will reveal specific weaknesses or limitations and it will provide a challenge to you to improve your program.

i. What is the quality of the school program?

Each school system must meet the educational needs of the community. This is the number-one priority in public relations. It should be noted, of course, that the public must make the major decisions regarding the development of the schools. Administrators may propose programs and offer suggestions, but only when the people have an understanding of the existing situation and a desire to alter it will significant changes take place. Public relations procedures, vital and necessary though they are, cannot substitute for the lack of quality in a school system. Here, then, is a fact which no administrator can forget: The world's best public relations program cannot hide a weak educational system.

II. Do citizens share in the planning and direction of the program?

Progress of education will continue through the combined efforts of competent staff members and interested citizens. Only through professional lay programs can the various aspects of school and community life be integrated. Every school system should have an advisory committee of citizens selected because of special interests or abilities, leadership qualities, and the capacity to work effectively with others. Such a group will require direction as well as suggestions from the superintendent. Its members must be oriented to their task. But the potential strength of such a group is great—far greater than many school administrators realize.

III. Is the program balanced?

It is easy to concentrate the public relations program on one or two big events during the year. You may defend this practice by saying, "Traditionally, these events are unique in our system. They have tremendous impact on public thought." You may be right. But don't neglect other phases of your program. Make the most of the three M's in public relations: men, media, and methods. Perhaps we should add another M: money.

IV. Are the objectives clear?

Much research precedes the planning of any campaign. When the facts are in, the administrator outlines strategies which he hopes will bring about increased understanding. What often passes for a program in public relations is in reality a collection of varied policies and techniques lacking direction. Appraisal of any program logically begins with a clarification of the aims and objectives.

v. Do you measure the results?

Broadly speaking, follow-up surveys are usually a combination of attitudes and opinions. Here again we find that people may give strange answers to questions. Indeed, their replies are often no measure of the factors sought. Mr. Blank's answers, for instance, may not be given in good faith. The research standard is raised somewhat when people tell of specific actions they took because of the influence of the public relations program. When a citizen says, "I certainly determined to do more for the schools when I read the editorial in the *Gazette*," the report can be considered accurate. To be safe, use tested scientific methods in your surveys of public opinion.

vi. What ideas are you trying to project into the public mind?

Make a comprehensive statement of the specific attitudes which you are trying to strengthen. School public relations policies are aimed at different segments of the public. Since each group has its unique characteristics, the competition for attention will differ as well as the channels of communication. In other words, start with facts, then dramatize them into compelling ideas.

vii. To whom are you directing your persuasive appeals?

Review everything you know about your public. If the information is meager and incomplete, by all means take time to amplify it. Learn everything you can about attitudes, income, occupations, educational levels, prejudices, and so on. You must know your public as individual human beings. You must know what they think, what prompts their attitudes. How can you make them accept your statements? The better you understand your public, the more effective will be your appeals.

viii. What is your competition?

List every appeal or activity that is immediately competitive. Describe each one fully and list the "selling" arguments of each.

146

Compare these arguments with your appeals, your special advantages, and your strategies. Finally, ask yourself, "Which argument would appeal to me?"

ix. Is the program tailor-made for local needs?

Each procedure in public relations must be geared to the particular community in which it is to operate. Therefore, each administrator must know his local conditions so that he can decide upon what level to focus his strategies. He must know the weaknesses in his program in order to strengthen his methods in those areas. If a school system has an outstanding public debt, for example, it is usually difficult to convince citizens that additional funds are needed for the schools. The alert superintendent knows the group attitudes of his community, their power, and their extent. Then he discovers the best way to fit his school promotion program to those attitudes.

x. Are staff members public relations–conscious?

Quite often the difference between the successful program and the one that fails is the attitude of the staff. A superintendent who directs an exceptionally fine public relations program has said, "Eternal, not spasmodic, education is a must in developing staff members." Teachers are and should always be the most important corps of good-will ambassadors for the system. If they are not, find and correct the basic errors of policy and practice. If they are, use every means to keep them so.

xi. Do public relations personnel have a voice in policy-making?

Every proposal and decision must be considered in the light of its effect on public relations. By the very nature of its scope and philosophy, public relations must be an administrative function. Frequently the superintendent summons businessmen, curricular experts, research personnel, and other authorities to talk over a problem. When they come to a decision the administrator calls in the public relations director or committee and says, "Here's what we've decided. Now tell the public about it." Successive decisions of this sort will upset the program. Remember that public relations personnel must have a voice in establishing policies.

xii. Do administrative leaders anticipate misunderstandings?

The old saying, "An ounce of prevention is worth a pound of cure," is most applicable to educational public relations. To use the definition of J. Carlisle MacDonald, "The public relations man should be looked upon as a safety engineer rather than a fire chief." This means that school administrators must be alert to any proposal, influence, or deed which may place the schools in jeopardy. Basically, educational policies must be made in the interest of the schools, the personnel, and the general public. When they are thoroughly understood by the masses, there is little danger of an adverse effect on public good will.

xiii. Are events and policies well timed?

Think for a moment of school systems which seem to lack public confidence. Often this state of affairs is caused by poor timing in public relations. Obviously, the time to correct an unforeseen misunderstanding is when it first occurs. Superintendents, teachers, and school board officials have lost many battles for public favor because they gave too little information too late. In most cases, public judgment is immediate. Be prepared to correct a misunderstanding at once.

xiv. Is the program co-ordinated?

Unity in any endeavor makes for strength. There is no duplication of effort when the superintendent defines all the interrelationships within his system. Certainly neither the superintendent nor his public relations workers can do all the work in building good will. But all policies should be considered in the light of their effect on public relations. All efforts to inform and interpret must have official clearance. The school administrator with a poorly organized program cannot expect increased public understanding, support, and co-operation. Co-ordination is the master key to efficiency in public relations.

xv. Is a wise choice made of techniques and channels?

Working with the modern media of communication, the leader of the public relations program brings ideas to the consciousness of his public. But he must do more than that. He must be concerned as well with achievements, services, needs, courses of action, ideals, objectives, beliefs, and the securing of public support for all of these.

In his public relations duties, the administrator is a practitioner with a wide range of instruments and a definite technique for their use. Always to be reckoned with is the fact that many procedures have potentialities which make their use both valuable and dangerous. Selection of a site for a new building, for example, may be announced in such a way as to bring criticism rather than support. It is always well, therefore, to estimate the consequences which are likely to result from the use of any idea or technique.

To get the best results from any tool of public relations, you must deal with it in terms of the specific function it performs. Too, it is well to know the requirements under which it performs at the particular time and place its use is required. If, for example, you wish to impress citizens with the vast amount of community services performed by school personnel, you may decide that an attractive, illustrated booklet would serve your purpose best.

Always subdivide the appeal of your subject and present it through a wide variety of avenues. In planning your campaign, outline your objectives and decide on the specific public units to which the message is to be directed. The next step should be to utilize existing avenues of approach, since people are more likely to accept ideas which come to them through regular channels.

The size of the school system naturally affects the range of the public relations program. In each case, the superintendent must make full use of available leadership and resources. A wise schoolman summed it up in this way: "Do the best you can with what you have."

xvɪ. Is the program dominated by a philosophy of service?

What is the most important factor in a successful public relations program? Media? Policies? Surveys? Competent personnel? Strategies? These are necessary, to be sure, but there is another element of more importance. It is the intangible spirit of service and enthusiasm that characterizes all school activities. It is loyalty and devotion; it is sacrificial work; it is the philosophy which drives men and women to give and not count the cost. It is the belief that life's dividends grow as they are shared. After all, the greatest element in public relations is not a word but a deed.

Citizen's Score Sheet
for Judging Public Schools[1]

What are the tangible qualities that make up a good school? *Life* staff writers, with the help of experts, devised a test by which an average citizen can tell just how good his school is. It was appraised by more than 150 school superintendents and was tested on more than five hundred good, average, and poor schools before its publication. In addition, its workability was analyzed and proved by the Educational Testing Service at Princeton, New Jersey. The test follows:

Answer
Yes or No

1. At least 60% of the parents are members of the PTA or other educationally active organizations. _____ _____

2. At least 50% of the members of the PTA or other educationally active organizations attend the general meetings. _____ _____

3. Teacher-parent conferences are arranged for a majority of the pupils. _____ _____

4. There are at least two teacher-parent conferences per year for *every* child. _____ _____

5. There are citizens present at all open school-board meetings. _____ _____

6. Public participation in local education has caused a significant change in the school within the last five years. _____ _____

[1] Reprinted by permission, *Life,* Vol. XXIX, No. 16 (October 16, 1950), 54–55. Copyright Time, Inc.

7. There has been a bond issue or tax levy extension voted within the last three years. ___ ___

8. At least 50% of the classroom teachers have masters' degrees. ___ ___

9. Teachers in the secondary school have at least one free period to every four teaching periods. ___ ___

10. Teachers in the elementary school have at least 40 minutes of rest period during the day ___ ___

11. The same wage scale exists for both elementary and secondary school teachers. ___ ___

12. The minimum starting salary for teachers is at least $2,700 a year. ___ ___

13. The possible top salary for classroom teachers is at least $4,000 a year. ___ ___

14. Instructors in high school vocational courses receive pay per week at least equal to the weekly wage of the trade they teach. ___ ___

15. The teachers and school staff are allowed sick leave with pay for at least 10 days annually. ___ ___

16. The school board contributes financial aid for inservice training of teachers. ___ ___

17. Teachers are paid and on duty at least a week before school opens. ___ ___

18. At least one written report per semester on each student is submitted by the teachers to the principal or parent supplementary to or replacing routine report cards. ___ ___

19. Courses comprising not less than 10% of the total curriculum have been added within the last five years. ___ ___

20. Laymen are used systematically to supplement classroom instruction both through consultation and actual participation. ___ ___

21. High school has vocational or industrial art courses. ___ ___

22. Employment in a part-time job is used systematically to supplement high school vocational training. _____ _____

23. Science courses include at least one hour of laboratory work for every four hours of classroom instruction. _____ _____

24. There is a kindergarten in the elementary school. _____ _____

25. In the elementary school pupils in the same grade are grouped according to reading levels and use different readers. _____ _____

26. The school makes use of a remedial reading specialist. _____ _____

27. All students study community, including techniques of local government, through visits and participation. _____ _____

28. The high school has an adult education program. _____ _____

29. There is a person specifically employed to work at least half time as a director of an adult education program. _____ _____

30. The chief administrative officer in the particular school is employed on a 12-month basis. _____ _____

31. The chief administrative officer in the particular school is free from teaching duties. _____ _____

32. The chief administrative officer in the particular school has engaged in professional study at a higher institution in the last five years. _____ _____

33. The chief administrative officer in the particular school is provided with full-time clerical help. _____ _____

34. The chief administrative officer in the particular school has a master's degree. _____ _____

35. The chief administrative officer in the particular school has secured advice from edu-

cation specialists other than state supervisors on his own initiative. ____ ____

36. In the elementary school there is an organized guidance program with a person at its head specifically responsible for its administration. ____ ____

37. In the high school, for every 250 students, there is at least one guidance councilor who is engaged in at least part-time activities with at least partial relief from teaching duties. ____ ____

38. There is a psychologist or psychiatrist available for consultation. ____ ____

39. At least $1.25 a year is spent on the school library for each pupil in the school's average daily attendance. ____ ____

40. A person trained in library techniques gives scheduled instruction in the use of a school library. ____ ____

41. At least $200 is spent per pupil. (Computed by dividing the total school budget for current operating expenditure by the total average daily attendance.) ____ ____

42. At least $4 was spent per pupil last year for textbooks and supplementary classroom reading material, excluding library books. ____ ____

43. At least 35c was spent last year per student in average daily attendance for audio-visual material, excluding purchase of basic projection and sound equipment. ____ ____

44. There is at least 30 square feet of floor area per classroom per pupil in average daily attendance. ____ ____

45. At least 80% of the classrooms have movable desks. ____ ____

46. The building is inspected yearly by an official fire or building authority. ____ ____

47. All the buildings are at least fire resistive. ____ ____
48. Fire drills are held at frequent intervals. ____ ____
49. The school custodian is a full-time member of the staff. ____ ____
50. The washing facilities have hot running water. ____ ____
51. There are flush toilets. ____ ____
52. The school supplies soap in the school lavatories. ____ ____
53. Students can obtain hot food at the school. ____ ____
54. There is a yearly medical examination of every student requiring at least 30 minutes per pupil to perform. ____ ____
55. The school provides inspection and cleaning of teeth by a dental hygienist at least once a year. ____ ____
56. There is a high school football field. ____ ____
57. There is a school gymnasium. ____ ____
58. There is an organized intramural athletic program in the high school. ____ ____
59. There is a club or hobby program. ____ ____
60. At least 65% of the pupils participate in voluntary club or hobby programs. ____ ____
61. Less than 10% of the students in either the eighth, ninth, 10th or 11th grades dropped out last year. ____ ____
62. A cumulative record is maintained on each student and it goes with him on transferring to a different school. ____ ____
63. The school board, through determining its own budget without restrictions, is independent of financial control by nonschool agencies of the municipal government. ____ ____

Total YES *Total* NO

HOW TO FIGURE SCHOOL'S SCORE

Add up the questions you have answered yes. Subtract from this the number you have answered no. Add the difference to 100 and compare it to the chart below.

	Elementary Schools	*High Schools*	*12-Grade Schools*
Best Schools Got	115–142	127–147	120–153
Average Schools Got	90–115	105–127	93–120
Worst Schools Got	45– 90	45–105	57– 93

A Check List to Help You Choose the Most Effective Channel of Communication

Advantages	*Disadvantages*

NEWSPAPERS:

Are most important medium in reaching the masses—Permit a wide variety of subjects —Are usually read by more than one person in family.	Are read hurriedly and thrown away—Are second to radio newscasts in popularity—Are not suited to some types of illustrations (because of rough newsprint)—Have limited color possibilities.

DIRECT MAIL:

Is a highly elastic medium—Has a personal touch—May be sent to homes—Offers a wide variety of forms—Permits tracing of results (through keys or coded systems).	May not reach recipient (mailing lists change rapidly)—May be offensive to recipient —May hinder rather than help (if copy is poorly prepared).

MAGAZINES:

Excel in color and make-up—Are read and reread—Are highly selective in relation to income and intelligence.	Are not flexible (copy is prepared months in advance)—Provide limited space—Lack local tie-in.

1 Adapted from *Public Relations for Churches* by Stewart Harral (New York, Abingdon-Cokesbury Press, 1945), 72–73.

OUTDOOR ADVERTISING:

Can be striking—Is seen by many people if location is good—Is attractive at night if illuminated—Permits use of color and movement—Is seen by many persons not reached through other channels.

Message may be too long to be seen in a flash—May have poor location—Demands frequent change of layout—May be overshadowed by adjacent advertising.

EXHIBITS:

Can tell an old story in a new way—Will attract persons of all classes and ages—Can convey ideas quickly and dramatically.

May result in confusion (from too many stimuli)—Cannot always have preferred position—May have restricted audience (due to weather and other factors).

RADIO:

Makes direct contact with large numbers of people—Is adapted to music, speech, and sound effects—Is more personal in appeal than printed words—Reaches most families —Is speediest of all media.

Must compete with network offerings—Script may be amateurish and ineffective—Permits no judging of size and response of audience—Must have script censored and edited.

SPEECHES:

Are well adapted to a personal, intimate message—Permit judging of audience reaction —May arouse enthusiasm for an idea and get immediate action — Permit audience to think along with speaker.

May be ill timed, too long, or inappropriate, or may have late spot on program—May be delivered by speaker with dull personality or distressing mannerisms, or one who may "unload" on audience.

TELEPHONE:

Is invaluable in reaching scores of people personally___ Gets immediate response___ May serve as reminder to attend meetings or induce other direct action.

May be used at wrong time (late at night or early morning)—Is ineffective if caller has unpleasant voice, talks too long, or uses an approach which is annoying.

PICTURES:

Tell a story quickly and dramatically—Treat a wide variety of subjects—Attract attention and cause comment—Appeal to those not interested in written matter.

Are ineffective unless made by professional photographer—May be too small, dull, or may lack animation and drama—May leave wrong idea.

PLAYS AND PAGEANTS:

Hold their audience if good and well acted—Make a deep impression—Lend variety to public relations program—Allow many people to participate—Give effective touch by using local cast.

Present difficulty of choosing suitable cast—Involve expense for good scenery, lighting effects, and properties—Are often amateurish in direction and production — Present problem of co-ordination in dealing with large groups.

MEETINGS AND CONVENTIONS:

Afford excellent opportunity to impress many persons— May be advertised by press, radio, and magazines—May enlist aid of many community agencies—Have good follow-up possibilities.

Demand intensive planning because of many details—May lack appealing program subjects—May occur at times inconvenient for majority of those invited—May lack proper advance promotion.

MOTION PICTURES:

Are usually presented in story form and are less boring than literature, speech, or radio—Appeal to all ages—Possess a power of emotional appeal that is basic in the educational process.

Require good equipment and competent operator—May be entertaining yet lack educational value—Are often unsuitable for individual instruction.

TELEVISION:

Makes intimate contact—Is adapted to music, speech, effects, as well as visual presentation—Offers opportunity to show certain phases of school life to great numbers—As long as medium has an element of something new, audience will watch sets for long periods of time—Offers unlimited variety of entertainment.

Requires undivided attention—Sets are usually limited for studio telecast—Like radio, eats up ideas rapidly—Cannot match live drama but is next best thing—Detailed planning is a must—Knowledge of lights, cameras, music, script, timing, acting, and other elements is essential in producing effective programs—Cost of set too expensive for masses.

Suggested Readings

California Association of School Administrators. *The People and the Schools of California*. Pasadena, Publication Press, 1950.

Child, Eleanor D., and Finch, Hardy R. *Producing School Movies*. Chicago, Committee on Standards for Motion Pictures and Newspapers of the National Council of Teachers of English, 1941.

Elicker, Paul E. (ed.) *Public Relations in Secondary Schools*. Washington, D. C., National Association of Secondary-School Principals, a department of the National Education Association, Vol. XXXII, Bulletin No. 152 (February, 1948).

Farley, Belmont. *School Publicity*. Stanford, Stanford University Press, 1934.

Fine, Benjamin. *Educational Publicity* (revised ed.). New York, Harper and Brothers, 1950.

Fisk, Robert S. *Public Understanding of What Good Schools Can Do*. New York, Teachers College, Columbia University, 1944.

Grinnell, John E. *Interpreting the Public Schools*. New York, McGraw-Hill Book Company, 1937.

Hand, Harold C. *What People Think About Their Schools*. New York, World Book Company, 1948.

Harral, Stewart. *Patterns of Publicity Copy*. Norman, University of Oklahoma Press, 1950.

Holmes, George H. (ed.) *Public Relations for Teacher Education*. Washington D. C., American Association of Colleges for Teacher Education, a department of the National Education Association, 1950.

Horn, Gunnar. *Public-School Publicity*. New York, Inor Publishing Company, Inc., 1948.

Moehlman, Arthur B. *Social Interpretation*. New York, D. Appleton-Century Company, Inc., 1938.

Mort, Paul R., and Vincent, William S. *A Look at Our Schools*. New York, The Ronald Press, 1946.

National Education Association (1201 Sixteenth Street, N. W., Washington 6, D. C.).

> *Building Public Confidence in the Schools*. Association for Supervision and Curriculum Development, 1949.
>
> *It Starts in the Classroom*. National School Public Relations Association, 1951.
>
> *Paths to Better Schools*. Twenty-third Yearbook. American Association of School Administrators, 1945.
>
> *Public Relations for America's Schools*. Twenty-eighth Yearbook. American Association of School Administrators, 1950.
>
> *School Boards in Action*. Twenty-fourth Yearbook. American Association of School Administrators, 1946.
>
> *Teacher and Public*. Eighth Yearbook. Department of Classroom Teachers, 1934.
>
> *The Public and the Elementary School*. Twenty-eighth Yearbook. Department of Elementary School Principals. Vol. XXIX, No. 1 (September, 1949).

Olsen, Edward G. *School and Community*. New York, Prentice-Hall, Inc., 1945.

————. *School and Community Programs*. New York, Prentice-Hall, Inc., 1949.

Reeder, Ward G. *An Introduction to Public-School Relations*. New York, The Macmillan Company, 1937.

————. *Campaigns for School Taxes*. New York, The Macmillan Company, 1946.

————. *School Boards and Superintendents*. New York, The Macmillan Company, 1946.

Rice, Arthur H. (ed.) *Today's Techniques*. Ann Arbor, Ann Arbor Press, 1943.

Rope, Frederick T. *Opinion Conflict and School Support*. Contributions to Education, No. 838. New York, Teachers College, Columbia University, 1941.

Sears, Jesse B. *Public School Administration*. New York, The Ronald Press, 1947.

Van Nice, C. R. *Teacher Teamwork With a Problem Public*. Topeka, Schools Activities Publishing Company, 1940.

Wade, Clarice (ed.). *Parent-Teacher Publicity*. Chicago, National Congress of Parents and Teachers, 1936.

Wiles, Kimball. *Supervision for Better Schools*. New York, Prentice-Hall, Inc., 1950.

Yauch, Wilbur A. *Improving Human Relations in School Administration*. New York, Harper and Brothers, 1949.

Yeager, William A. *School-Community Relations* (revised ed.). New York, The Dryden Press, 1951.

Index

FALVEY MEMORIAL LIBRARY
VILLANOVA UNIVERSITY

DATE DUE

04. 01. 75 DISCHARGED	JUN 28 '88 DISCHARGED
08. 19. 75 DISCHARGED	
DISCHARGED	
12. 76 DISCHARGED	
DISCHARGED	
02. 01. 78	
02. 21. 78	
04. 11. 78	